BIBLE STITCHERY

BIBLE STITCHERY

Judith Schoener Kalina

A DOUBLEDAY-GALILEE ORIGINAL
Doubleday & Company, Inc., Garden City, New York, 1980

Unless otherwise noted biblical excerpts are taken from The Jerusalem Bible ©
1966 by Darton, Longman, & Todd, Ltd., and Doubleday & Company, Inc. Used
by permission of the publisher

Library of Congress Catalog Card Number: 79-8934
ISBN: 0-385-14966-2

Copyright © 1980 by Judith Schoener Kalina

ALL RIGHTS RESERVED
PRINTED IN THE UNITED STATES OF AMERICA

9 8 7 6 5 4 3 2

To my dear parents, Harry and Rose Schoener,
and to my dear mother-in-law, Tillie Kalina.

Acknowledgments

This book could never have come to fruition without the efforts of many people. Special thanks to Margaret A. Brown who copied over all my little scribbled dots and lines and made from them civilized and presentable graphed designs. Grateful thanks to my dear friend Vivian Chiprut Nahmias who rescued me by typing a manuscript which only a trained intelligence agent could decode. Love and much gratitude to my wonderful family: to my husband, David, who encouraged me with love and patience and who helped edit the manuscript; to my children, Nora and Jenny, who patiently waited for suppers or made them themselves, and who helped with criticism and good suggestions. Thanks to Florence Bence, Bano Carlos, Jean Covington, Dorothy Crosby, Mary Ann Raph, Eve Roshevsky, Carole Schwartz, Jan Waring, and Donna Rothchild who worked the designs into full-blown pieces. Further thanks to Leslie Ann Gelber for color and stitch suggestions and to Esther Becker of Sunray Yarns for yarn and canvas selections. Thanks to art director Diana Klemin who encouraged me with the designs and gave fine aesthetic criticism. Last, but not least, special thanks and affection to my patient, hard-working editor, Evelyn Bence, who was there from the very beginning of the project to the very end and who supported and encouraged me throughout.

Contents

INTRODUCTION
- TRANSFERRING THE DESIGN — 1
- ALTERING THE SCALE — 1
- NEEDLEPOINT STITCHES — 2
- EMBROIDERY STITCHES — 6
- MATERIALS — 7
- TECHNIQUES — 8
- BLOCKING — 8
- FINISHING PROJECTS — 8

PROJECTS
1. "Sing Unto the Lord" (Wall Hanging) — 12
2. Alpha and Omega (Change Purse) — 13
3. Stork (Eyeglass Case) — 14
4. Garden of Eden (Pillow) — 16
5. Dove (Evening Purse) — 18
6. Noah's Ark (Cross-stitch Bib) — 20
7. Noah's Ark (Pillow) — 24
8. Ram's Head (Change Purse) — 25
9. Abraham (Wall Hanging) — 27
10. Jacob's Ladder (Wall Hanging) — 29
11. Joseph's Dream (Pillow) — 31
12. Camel (Bib) — 34
13. Burning Bush (Pillow) — 36
14. Moses and Ten Commandments (Wall Hanging) — 38
15. Naomi and Ruth (Pillow) — 40
16. David with Harp (Pillow) — 42
17. "The Lord Is My Shepherd" (Wall Plaque) — 44
18. Family Tree (Wall Plaque) — 48
19. The Horseman (Rug) — 49
20. Eagle (Wall Hanging) — 51
21. Jonah in the Fish (Pillow) — 54
22. Lion (Christmas Ornament) — 58
23. Ezekiel's Wheel (Pillow) — 60
24. "Kindly Words" (Wall Plaque) — 62
25. Mary and Baby (Birth Announcement) — 64

26.	Star (Christmas Ornament)	66
27.	Wise Men on Camels (Banner)	68
28.	King (Christmas Ornament)	70
29.	Camel (Christmas Ornament)	72
30.	"Give Us This Day" (Toaster Cover)	74
31.	The Good Shepherd (Wall Plaque)	76
32.	Lilies (Tote Bag)	80
33.	Jesus Calming the Waters (Wall Plaque)	81
34.	Waterpot (Pillow)	84
35.	Fish (Tote)	86
36.	Jesus and the Children (Wall Plaque)	88
37.	Prodigal Son (Banner)	90
38.	Pentecost (Wall Plaque)	92
39.	Heaven's Gates (Plaque)	94
40.	"When Thou Liest Down" (Wall Plaque)	98
Bibliography		99

BIBLE STITCHERY

INTRODUCTION

We who love to create needlework are always in search of new ideas and materials. Our files are crammed; our bookshelves overflowing. And to meet the demands for new designs, magazines, newspapers, and books constantly churn out new stitchery projects. It has always amazed me that, in all this profusion of ideas, the Bible is rarely represented. The Bible is one of the richest sources of sheer visual and intellectual excitement. What could be more natural than translating this wonderful book into the handcrafted artifacts with which we live.

Bible Stitchery illustrates original designs in needlepoint and cross-stitch based on specific biblical themes and stories.

In the introductory chapter, the book contains specific instructions on how to transfer designs, how to alter scale, various needlepoint and cross-stitch techniques, and instructions for certain types of projects. The remainder of the book presents the designs and projects themselves and, at the end, there is a short bibliography for further reference.

TRANSFERRING THE DESIGN

All of the projects are drawn on a grid to facilitate transferring the designs to canvas or fabric. The grid will also help to adapt designs for different projects and facilitates enlarging or reducing the designs.

Each square on the design grid is equal to one mesh on the canvas. Count the squares to find out how many spaces to work in each color. In this way, depending upon the size of the mesh, it will be easy to enlarge or reduce the design or keep it close to the size of the original.

Trace the design onto the canvas with colorfast markers or thinned acrylic paints.

For cross-stitch, transfer the design by marking the cloth with a pencil.

ALTERING THE SCALE

There are several ways to enlarge or reduce a design or to use only one segment of it. One way is to transfer the original design onto another piece of graph paper, proportionally increasing or decreasing the number of squares. For example, to double the size of the design, one square inch of the original might be equal to two square inches of graph paper. The converse holds true to reduce the design.

A second method is to copy the original drawing onto a grid where the squares are of a different size. Here, the grid contains the same number of squares, but the size of the squares is altered to enlarge or reduce the design. Thus, if the project is to be larger than the design, a larger grid would be chosen; if the finished piece is to be smaller, a smaller grid would be chosen. The original is copied, square by square, onto the new paper.

The simplest way to alter the size of a design is to have a photostat made by a printer. Trace the original outline onto tracing paper. Give it to a printer, telling him the size needed for the finished design, and he will produce an enlarged or reduced photostat according to the specifications. The photostat can then be traced onto the canvas.

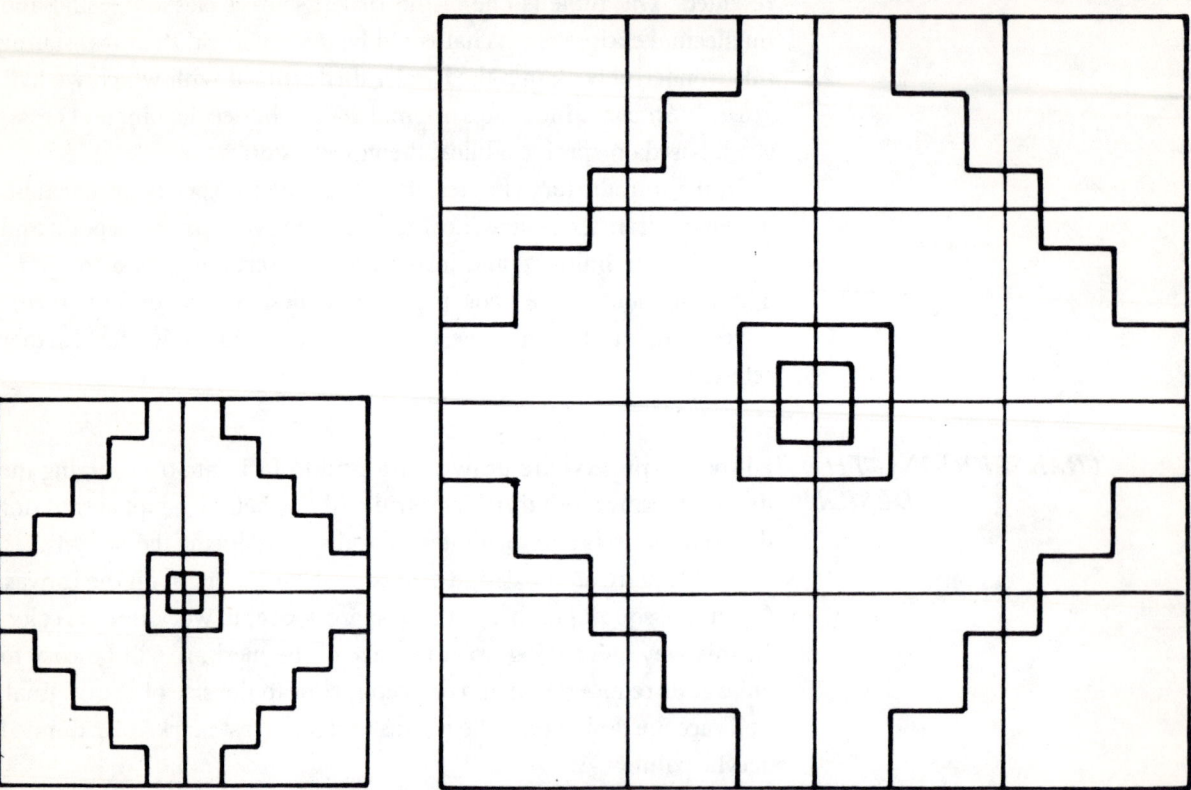

Figure 1: Grid Method For Altering Scale

NEEDLEPOINT STITCHES

There is a great deal of variation in needlework just in the selection of stitches. Indeed, the unique quality of each project will depend greatly on the choice of stitches. Use the ones suggested in this book or refer to those books listed in the bibliography for a broader stitch vocabulary. For the background of the projects, use the basket-weave or continental stitch, and then use some of the other stitches for variation. For smaller areas, like facial features and outlines, use surface embroidery such as French knots or the running stitch.

The continental stitch requires working the first row from right to left, then turning the canvas completely upside down and working the second row from right to left. For row three, invert the canvas and start all over again.

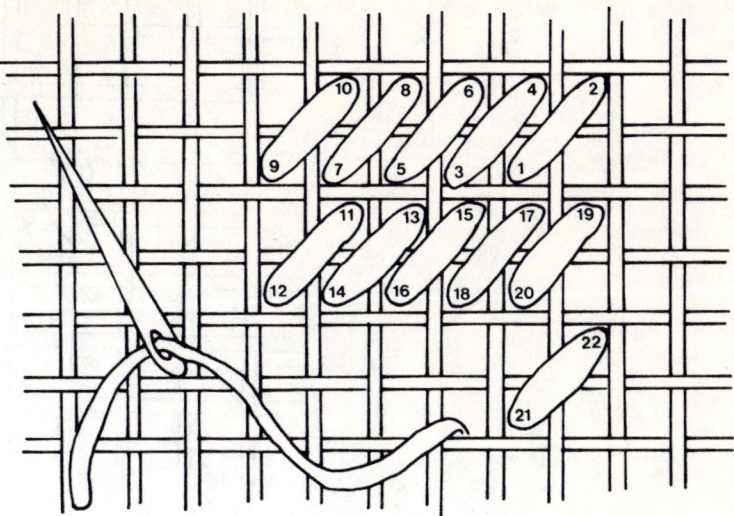

Figure 2: The Continental Stitch

The basket-weave stitch does not require turning the canvas. It is a sturdy stitch and the one least likely to distort the canvas. Each stitch is worked from bottom to top and diagonally to the right. Each hole is used twice.

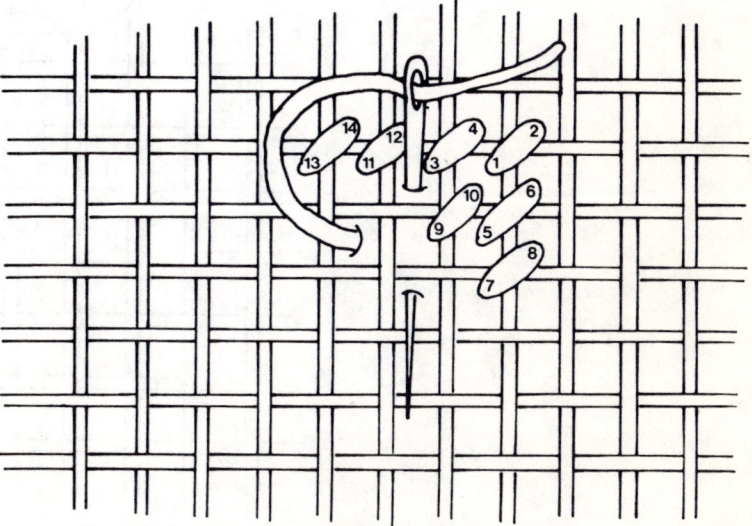

Figure 3: The Basket Weave Stitch

3

On the surface of the needlepoint the half cross-stitch looks like the continental stitch, but it uses less wool and is faster to work.

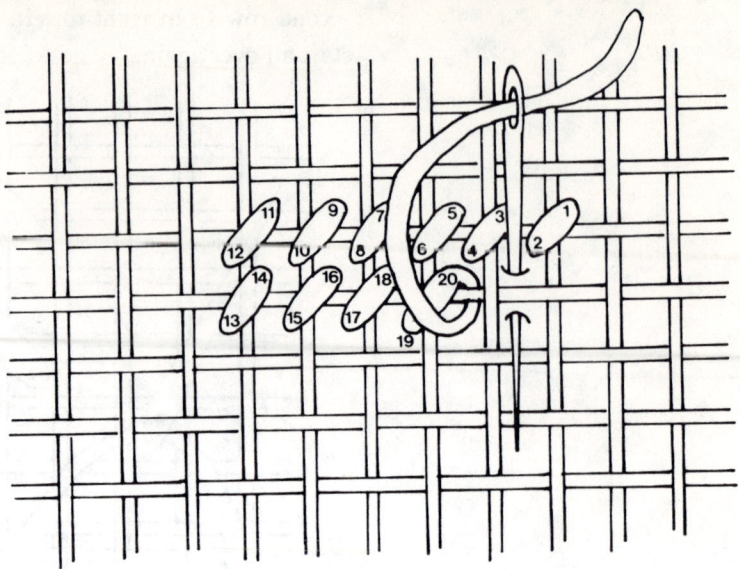

Figure 4: The Half Cross-Stitch

The cross-stitch can be used for canvas embroidery, but is generally used for working on even-weave fabric. This stitch is based on the half cross-stitch. Work one row of half cross-stitches from left to right and then complete the cross by working the same row from right to left.

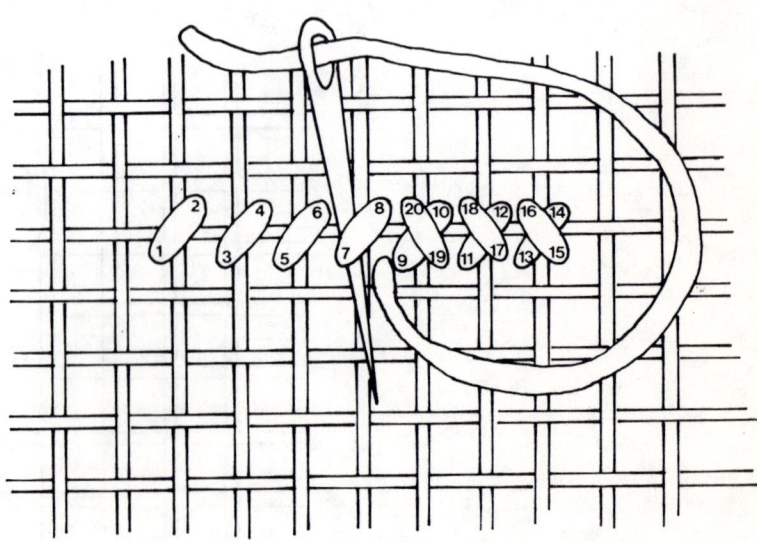

Figure 5: The Cross-Stitch

The upright Gobelin is an upright or vertical stitch. Come up at one, go down at two, come up at three, go down at four, and so on. To make the next row, the top of the stitches go into the same holes formed by the bottom of the first row.

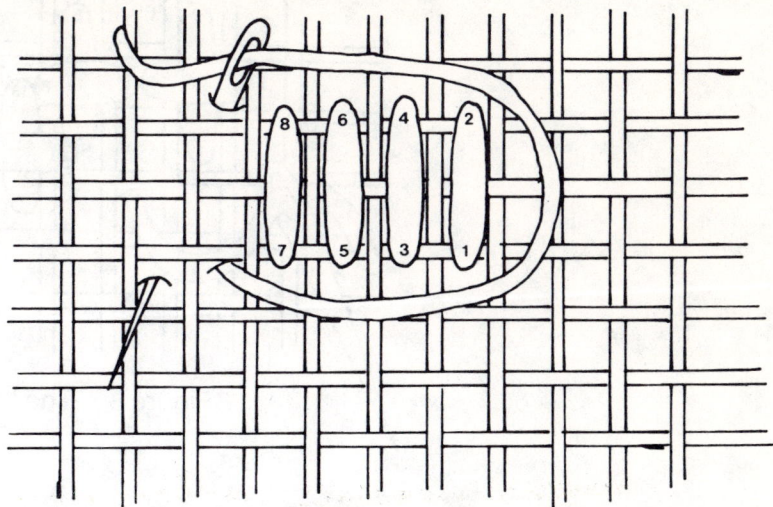

Figure 6: The Upright Gobelin Stitch

The mosaic is a diagonal stitch of one long and two short stitches. Follow the numbers for the direction of working.

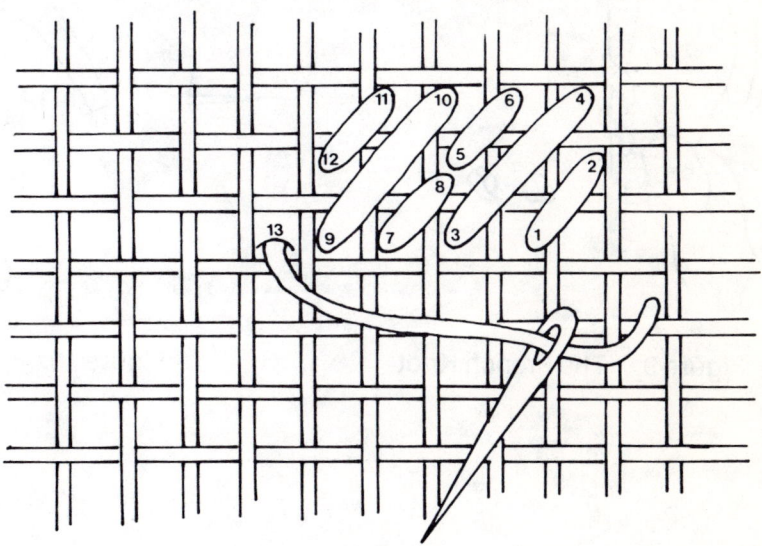

Figure 7: The Mosaic Stitch

In the upright cross-stitch, each stitch is completed before going on to the next one. At the end of each row, turn the canvas upside down and continue.

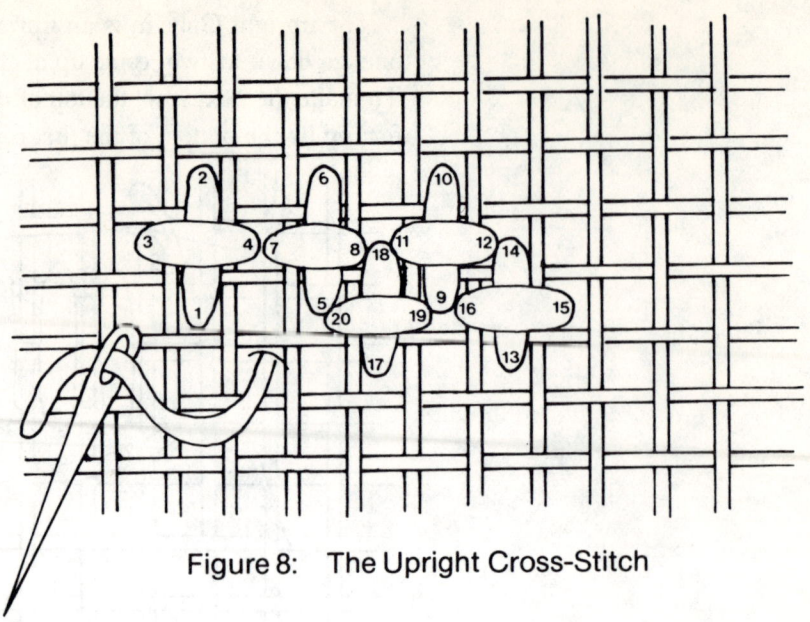

Figure 8: The Upright Cross-Stitch

EMBROIDERY STITCHES

The French knot is used for special accents and textures in counted thread as well as in free embroidery.

To create a definite line, use the back stitch.

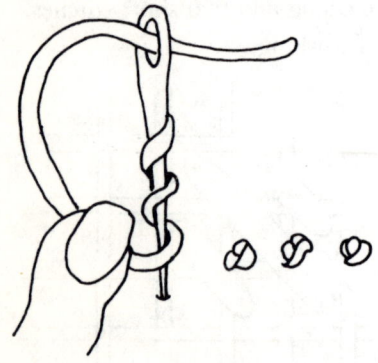

Figure 9: The French Knot

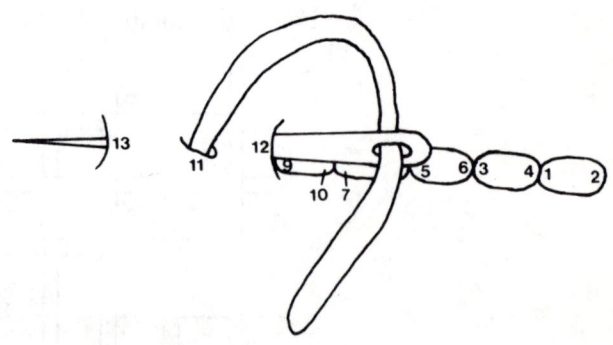

Figure 10: The Back Stitch

Use the blind stitch for finishing.

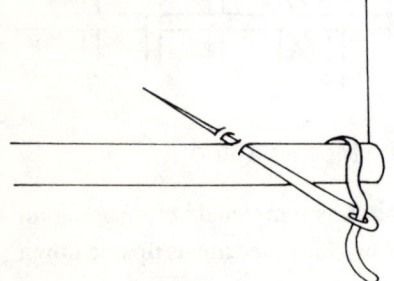

Figure 11: The Blind Stitch

MATERIALS

Canvas Needlepoint projects require either single-thread (mono canvas), double-thread (Penelope), or plastic canvas. These canvases are available in a variety of mesh sizes. Special rug canvas, also in varying mesh sizes, can be obtained for making a rug. To estimate the amount of canvas to purchase, first count the number of squares on the design and then divide by the number of canvas meshes per square inch. For example, if there are sixty squares across in the design, and the canvas mesh is ten-mesh-to-the-inch, the project will measure six inches across. If the canvas mesh is twelve-to-the-inch, the piece will be only five inches across. To allow for mounting and stretching and other finishing techniques, a seam allowance of three inches all around must be added. This may seem excessive, but it can help correct any miscalculation.

Cross-stitch Cloth Cross-stitch projects are best done on aida cloth, an even-weave fabric manufactured specifically for this technique. Hardanger, linen, or gingham can also be used. Unlike needlepoint, only the design is filled in; the background is left unstitched. The size of the finished piece must be decided upon, then the amount of cloth needed is determined by counting the squares in the design and dividing by the number of meshes-per-square-inch on the fabric.

Yarns and Embroidery Floss Persian wool, tapestry wool, and rug yarn are the most commonly used needlepoint yarns. These are purchased after the canvas has been chosen, as they must be matched to the mesh size. To estimate the amounts to purchase, work up a one-inch square, keeping track of how much yarn is used. For an approximate figure, multiply that by the number of square inches there are of each color. Always overbuy because dye lots differ and colors may be difficult to match on a repurchase.

For cross-stitch projects, embroidery floss is the best choice.

All of the projects in *Bible Stitchery* were worked on DMC tapestry wool or pearl cotton. The color codes are keyed to these products. However, you may make your choice based upon what is available locally.

Needles Needle choice is dependent upon the canvas and the yarn. Tapestry needles are used for canvas work. This needle has a blunt point and a long eye and comes in a variety of sizes. Embroidery or crewel needles are used for embroidery work. These also come in a variety of sizes.

The best way to choose is to be sure that the needle can easily pass through the canvas and that its eye is large enough to accommodate the thread or yarn.

TECHNIQUES To begin a needlepoint project, measure the canvas. Mark the margin of the design with a waterproof marker. Making sure to add three inches for seam allowance all the way around, cut the canvas to size. Bind the cut edges of the canvas with masking tape. If someone else is going to finish the piece (for example, if it is going to be upholstered onto a chair), obtain a paper pattern from that person. Draw the design onto the canvas with a marker. To color the different sections on the mesh, use thinned acrylic paints.

It is best to sew from the center out. Mark the center of the canvas. If the canvas is large, roll in the top and bottom and pin them, leaving space to work.

Thread the needle with an eighteen-inch length of yarn. While sewing, maintain a consistent tension: do not pull too tight or too loose. If a mistake is made and it is necessary to rip out some stitches, unthread the needle and pull the stitches out with the back of the needle. For larger areas, cut the stitches with small sharp scissors and pull out the thread with a pair of tweezers.

When beginning or ending a stitch, do not make a knot. To begin a stitch, leave a one-inch tail. Hold it in the direction of the stitching. Then, work the first few stitches over and around it.

To end a strand, weave approximately one inch of yarn through the stitches in the back. Clip closely.

BLOCKING To get it back to its true shape, the finished canvas should be blocked. This can be done commercially, or it can be done at home. Dampen the canvas by rolling it in a wrung-out bath towel. Let it sit for several hours. Cover a flat wooden board with a piece of brown wrapping paper. Mark the outline and shape of the finished piece in pencil. Lay the damp piece out on the board and, by using rustproof tacks, pull and tug the canvas into shape, first tacking it in the center of opposite sides and then out from there. Let the canvas dry thoroughly.

Block a cross-stitch project in the same manner.

FINISHING PROJECTS Each type of work is finished differently. For a pillow, cut the backing fabric the same size as the blocked canvas. Facing right sides together, sew around the edges leaving a section of the edge open. Clip the edges, turn and stuff, and, using a blind stitch, close up the open edge.

Figure 12: Mitering Corners

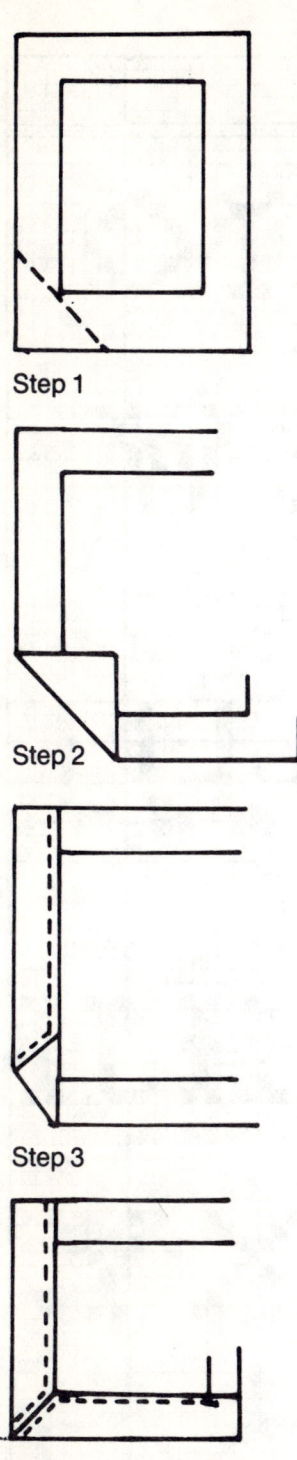

Step 1

Step 2

Step 3

Step 4

To finish a stitched picture as a framed wall piece, first decide on the dimensions by purchasing packaged precut frame pieces. These are available in hardware, hobby, or art-supply stores. The frame should approximate the size of the design. Later, if you wish to cover the stitchery with a piece of glass, it is easy to have one cut to size.

Stretch the back of the blocked fabric around quarter-inch plywood which has been cut to the size of the design. First tack the centers, making sure the design is centered. Continue stretching and tacking it every inch or so around. Then miter the corners.

A needlepoint picture can also be hung as a banner. After blocking, cut a piece of linen a half inch smaller on all sides than the finished hanging. Baste this to the back of the canvas. Fold the edges of the finished work over the lining, miter the corners, and blind-stitch it down. Steam lightly. Sew evenly spaced loops of needlepoint or linen to the top of the picture. Cut a piece of silk or some other suitable lining one inch larger on all sides than the hanging. Blind-stitch this to the back of the hanging. Steam lightly. Slip a rod or dowel through the loops and suspend from the wall with fishline and hooks.

A pillow or tote bag design can be adapted to a chair cushion or footstool. Take the seat off the chair or stool and measure carefully before beginning the project. Then trace your design and work up the needlepoint. After blocking, size the piece and leave the extra canvas in place. Attach the needlework to the seat with nails and then reattach the seat to the chair.

Occasionally, small areas or motifs from a larger design can be isolated and used independently. A project like a pincushion or bookmark is suitable for small designs. To make a pincushion, follow the general suggestions for a pillow. For a bookmark, bind the raw edges with bias tape.

To finish a rug, clip the canvas edges of the blocked piece to one inch all around. With carpet thread, overcast rug binding to the top of the canvas along the edge of the design. Fold the binding tape under and overcast it to the back of the rug. Steam lightly. Do not line the rug; place a rug pad under it.

The following projects are accompanied by stitch and color suggestions. You can make them as suggested or vary them in any way that is suitable. Change the color or stitches. Add a border or drop a border. Take out a small section and use it for a small project. Whatever you do will be your own unique expression.

PROJECTS

SING UNTO

A NEW

ABCDEFGHIJK

RSTUVWXY

ijKlmnopqrst

THE LORD
SONG

KLMNOPQ,
Zabcdefgh
uvwxyz...?

1

"Sing Unto the Lord" (Wall Hanging)

Sing unto the Lord a new song, and his praise from the end of the earth...

Isaiah 42:10 KJV (King James Version).

SUGGESTED PROJECTS needlepoint wall piece, needlepoint pillow.

ADDITIONAL SUGGESTIONS cross-stitch wall piece.

SUGGESTED STITCHES basket weave or continental; use surface embroidery to outline the staff.

Graph 1

☐ 7434 yellow

⊡ 7971 buttercup

■ 7708 purple

12

2

Alpha and Omega (Change Purse)

And then he said, "It is already done. I am the Alpha and the Omega, the Beginning and the End. I will give water from the well of life free to anybody who is thirsty."

Revelation 21:6.

SUGGESTED PROJECTS needlepoint change purse or pincushion.

SUGGESTED STITCHES basket weave or continental.

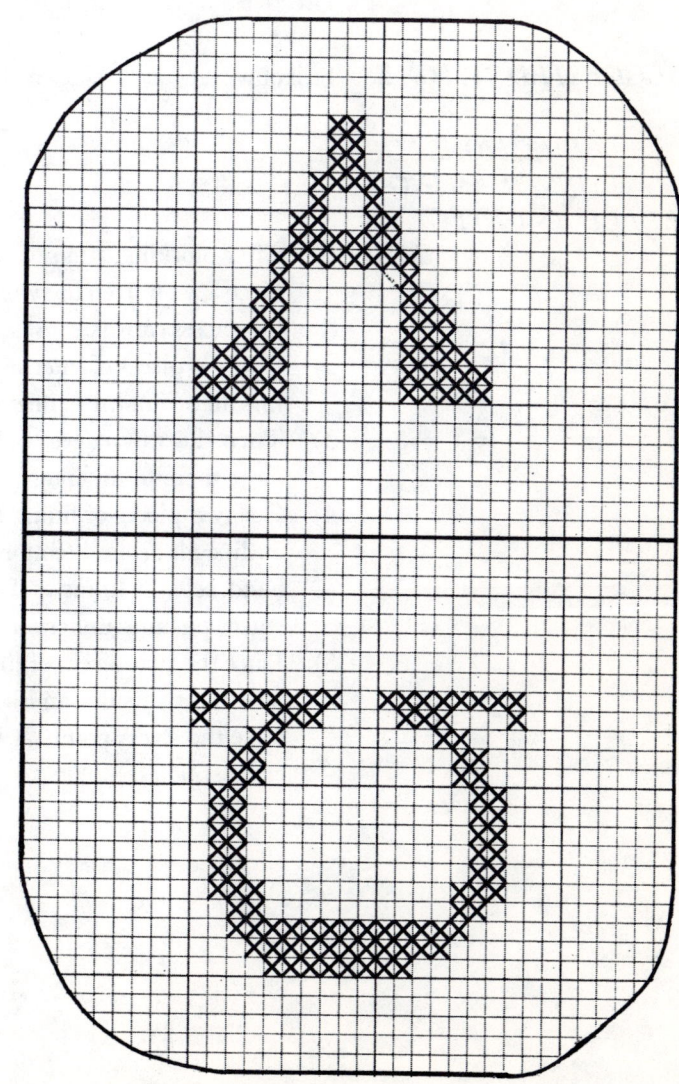

Graph 2

☒ 7341 bright green

☐ 7257 magenta

For directions to make a change purse, see RAM'S HEAD, Graph #8.

13

3

Stork (Eyeglass Case)

The trees of Yahweh get rain enough,
those cedars of Lebanon he planted;
here the little birds build their nest
and, on the highest branches, the stork has its home.

Psalm 104:16–17.

SUGGESTED PROJECTS   needlepoint eyeglass case.

ADDITIONAL SUGGESTIONS   The stork design is for one side; on the other side, initials would be effective.

SUGGESTED STITCHES   basket weave; use surface embroidery to outline the stork's legs.

DIRECTIONS FOR CONSTRUCTING A NEEDLEPOINT EYEGLASS CASE

1) After blocking, run several rows of machine stitching around the piece ½ inch from the worked area of the needlepoint. Trim away the excess canvas.
2) Cut two pieces of interfacing ¼ inch smaller then the original outline all around. Pin one of these to the wrong side of each piece.
3) Turn the raw edges of the canvas over on the wrong side and baste them to the interfacing.
4) Cut two pieces of lining material ½ inch larger than the original outline all around (cotton and silk are good lining materials). By hand, sew the lining to the wrong sides of both pieces with a blind stitch, pushing under all seam allowances.
5) Place the two pieces of lined canvas together, wrong sides facing. Sew the two sides and bottom together. You may want to reinforce the stress points at both sides of the top opening by taking extra stitches.

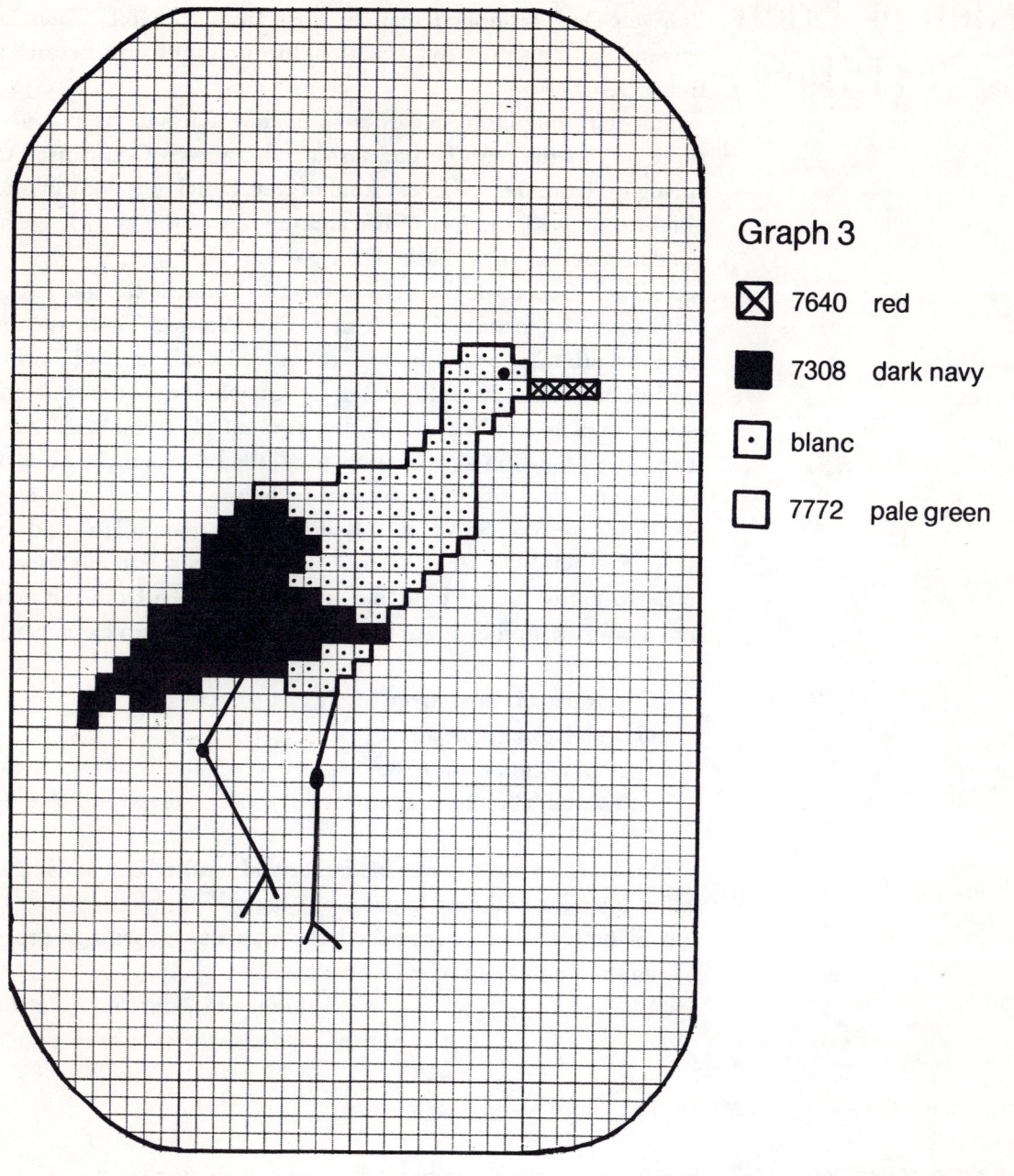

4

Garden of Eden (Pillow)

Yahweh God fashioned man of dust from the soil. Then he breathed into his nostrils a breath of life, and thus man became a living being.

Yahweh God planted a garden in Eden which is in the east, and there he put the man he had fashioned. Yahweh God caused to spring up from the soil every kind of tree, enticing to look at and good to eat, with the tree of life and the tree of the knowledge of good and evil in the middle of the garden.

Yahweh God took the man and settled him in the garden of Eden to cultivate and take care of it. Then Yahweh God gave the man this admonition, "You may eat indeed of all the trees in the garden. Nevertheless of the tree of the knowledge of good and evil you are not to eat, for on the day you eat of it you shall most surely die." The man gave names to all the cattle, all the birds of heaven and all the wild beasts. But no helpmate suitable for man was found for him. So Yahweh God made the man fall into a deep sleep. And while he slept, he took one of his ribs and enclosed it in flesh. Yahweh God built the rib he had taken from the man into a woman, and brought her to the man. The man exclaimed:

"This at least is bone from my bones,
and flesh from my flesh!
this is to be called woman,
for this was taken from man."

This is why a man leaves his father and mother and joins himself to his wife, and they become one body.

Now both of them were naked, the man and his wife, but they felt no shame in front of each other.

Genesis 2:7–9, 15–17, 20–25.

SUGGESTED PROJECTS   pillow, framed wall piece, tote bag.

SUGGESTED STITCHES   basket weave, upright cross-stitch, mosaic, chain stitch.

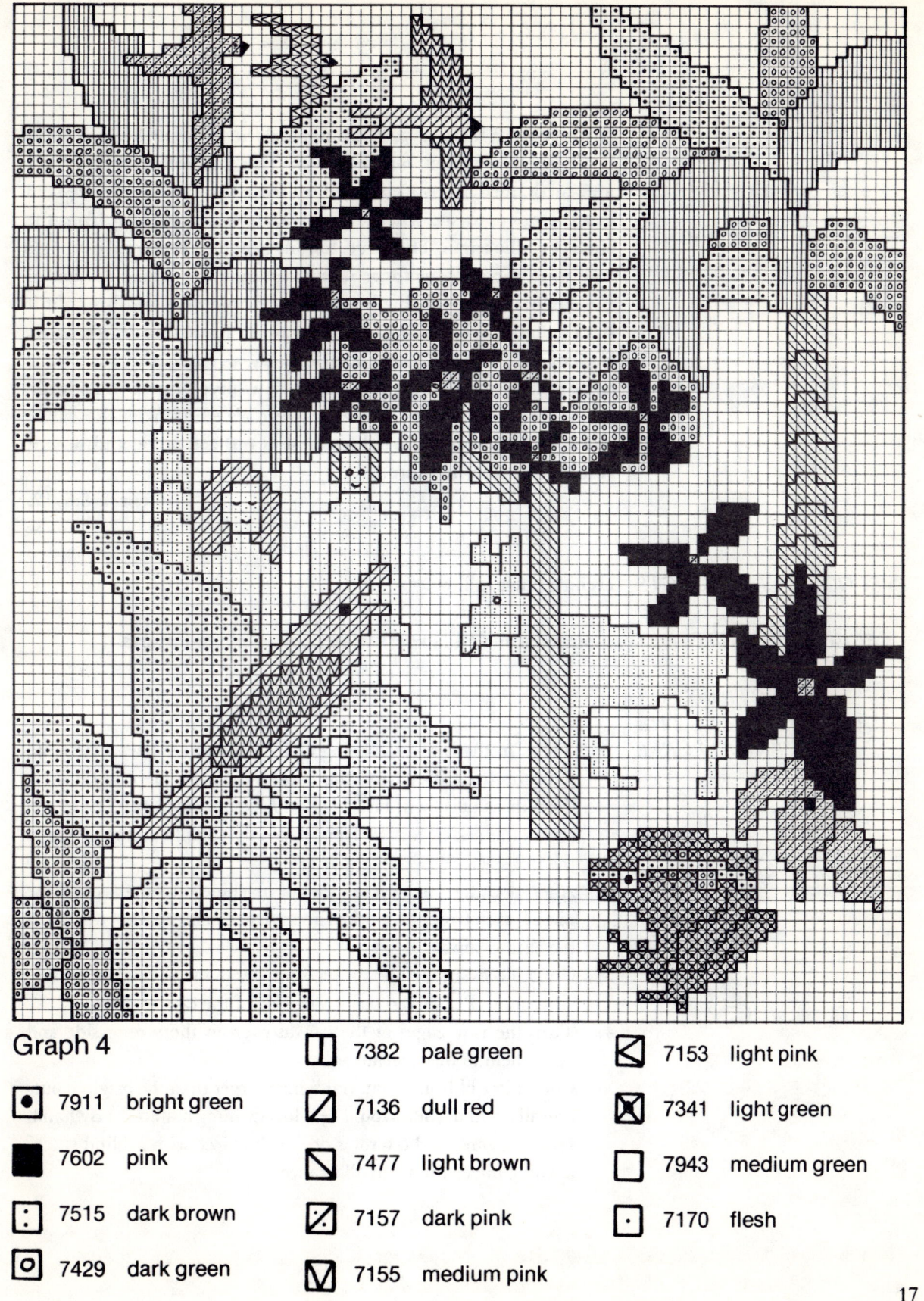

Graph 4

Symbol	Code	Color
⊡	7911	bright green
■	7602	pink
⊡	7515	dark brown
⊙	7429	dark green
⏛	7382	pale green
⧄	7136	dull red
⧅	7477	light brown
⧄	7157	dark pink
⋈	7155	medium pink
⊠	7153	light pink
⊠	7341	light green
□	7943	medium green
·	7170	flesh

5

Dove (Evening Purse)

At the end of forty days Noah opened the porthole he had made in the ark and he sent out the raven. This went off, and flew back and forth until the waters dried up from the earth. Then he sent out the dove, to see whether the waters were receding from the surface of the earth. The dove, finding nowhere to perch, returned to him in the ark, for there was water over the whole surface of the earth; putting out his hand he took hold of it and brought it back into the ark with him. After waiting seven more days, again he sent out the dove from the ark. In the evening, the dove came back to him and there it was with a new olive branch in its beak. So Noah realized that the waters were receding from the earth. After waiting seven more days he sent out the dove, and now it returned to him no more.

Genesis 8:6–12.

SUGGESTED PROJECTS   evening purse, pillow.

SUGGESTED STITCHES   continental and Milanese; surface embroidery for features.

DIRECTIONS FOR CONSTRUCTING THE EVENING PURSE

1) Think of the canvas as being divided into three parts: the front flap, the front itself, and the back. When the piece is finished, these three parts will be folded over like an envelope. The graph shows the design for the front flap only. Triple this to arrive at the full size.
2) After blocking, run several rows of machine stitching around the piece ½ inch from the worked area of the needlepoint. Trim away the excess canvas.
3) Cut a piece of interfacing ¼ inch smaller than the original outline all around. Pin this to the wrong side of the canvas piece.
4) Turn the raw edges of the canvas over on the wrong side and baste them to the interfacing.
5) Cut a piece of lining material ½ inch larger than the original outline all around. (Silk would be a lovely lining material.) By hand, sew the lining to the wrong side of the piece with a blind stitch, pushing under the seam allowance.

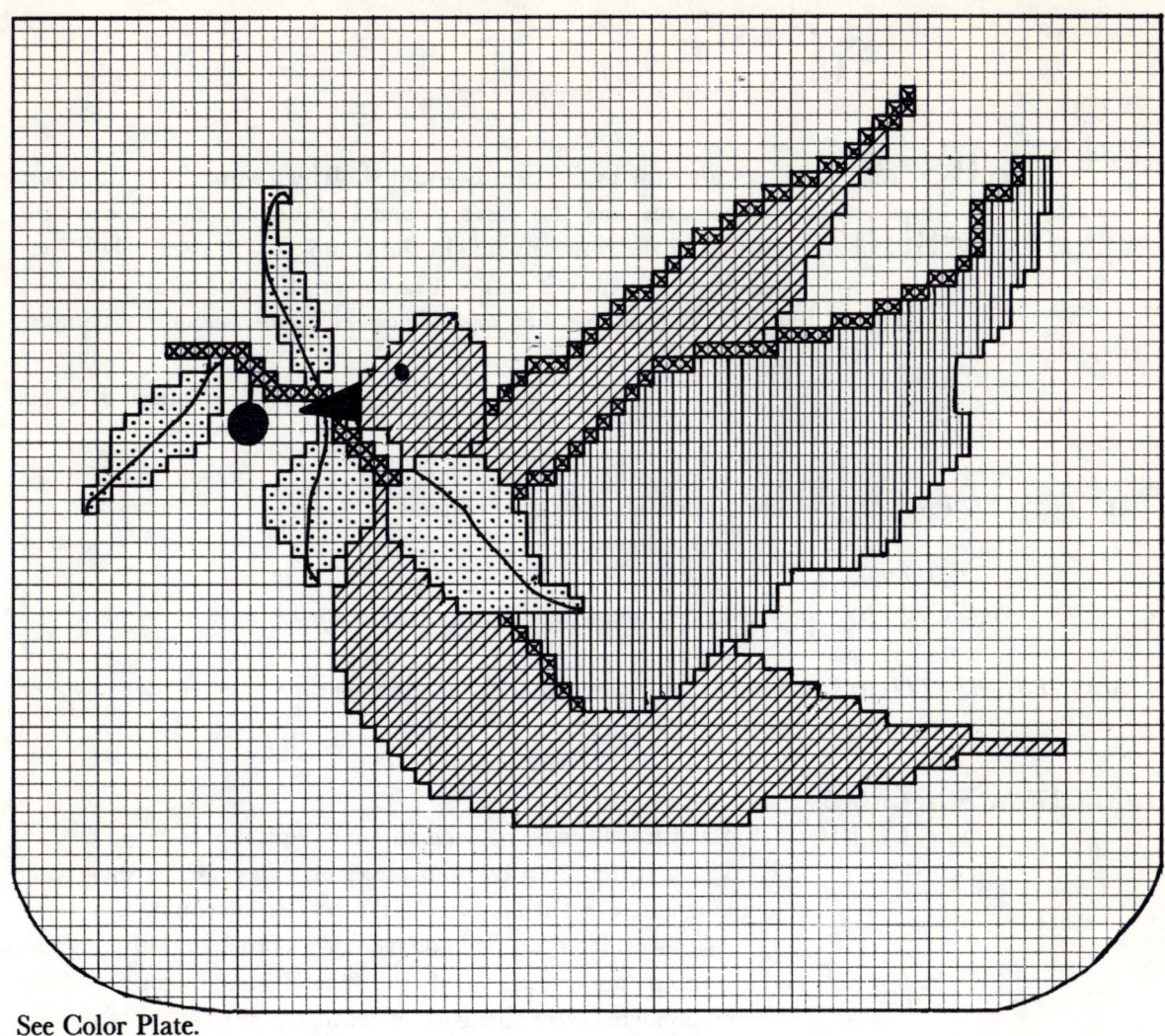

See Color Plate.

Graph 5

- ☐ 7207 dull red
- ◩ blanc
- ⫼ 7280 beige
- ⊡ 3345 medium green (DMC perle)
- ⊠ 7499 green
- ■ black
- ⊠ silver lame

6) With wrong sides facing, fold over the piece to make an envelope. Give it a light steaming. Sew the sides of the purse with a blind stitch.
7) Use as a clutch purse or sew on straps made of fancy satin cording. Add a few beads for a decorative effect.

6

Noah's Ark (Cross-stitch Bib)

I set my bow in the clouds and it shall be a sign of the Covenant between me and the earth. When I gather the clouds over the earth and the bow appears in the clouds, I will recall the Covenant between myself and you and every living creature of every kind. And so the waters shall never again become a flood to destroy all things of flesh.

Genesis 9:13–15.

SUGGESTED PROJECTS
: cross-stitch bib, cross-stitch plaque.

ADDITIONAL SUGGESTIONS
: needlepoint pillow, needlepoint tote.

SUGGESTED STITCHES
: cross-stitch, French knots for features; outline chimney, windows and leaf with No. 311.

DIRECTIONS FOR CROSS-STITCH BIB

1) Enlarge pattern by copying on 1-inch square grid.
2) Using pattern, cut two bib pieces of aida cloth, hardanger, or gingham. Cut one bib piece of flannel (for interlining).
3) After working design on one piece of embroidery cloth, place all three pieces together, with the flannel in the center and the embroidered piece facing up. Baste together.
4) Using bias tape, bind the sides together.
5) Bind the neck edge with bias tape. Leave a 9-inch tail on both sides for ties.
6) Sew the long ends of the ties, and knot the ends.

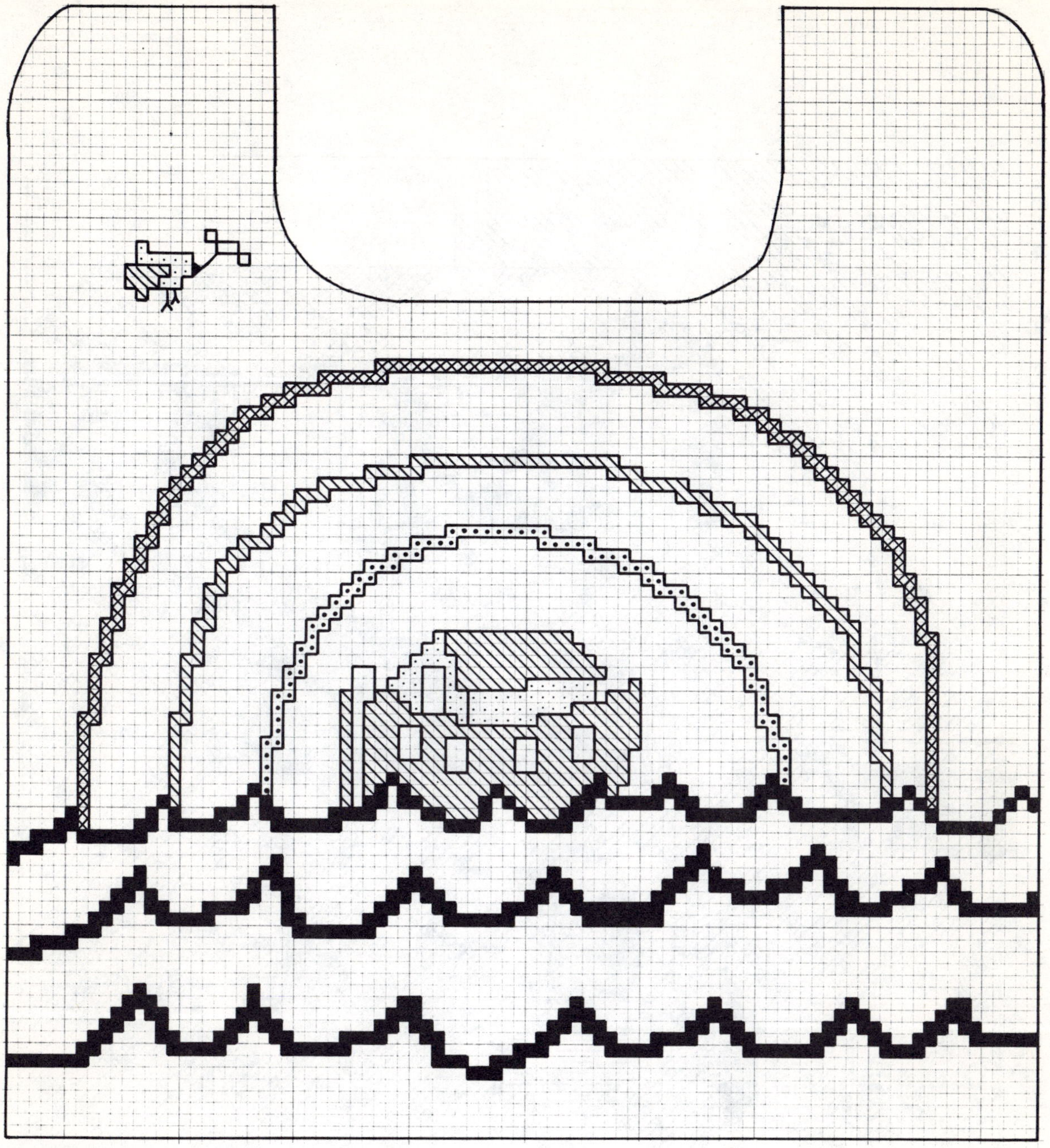

Graph 6

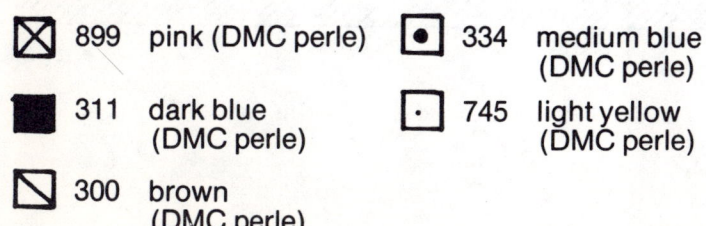

⊠ 899 pink (DMC perle)
■ 311 dark blue (DMC perle)
◨ 300 brown (DMC perle)
⊡ 334 medium blue (DMC perle)
⊡ 745 light yellow (DMC perle)

See Color Plate.

Graph 7

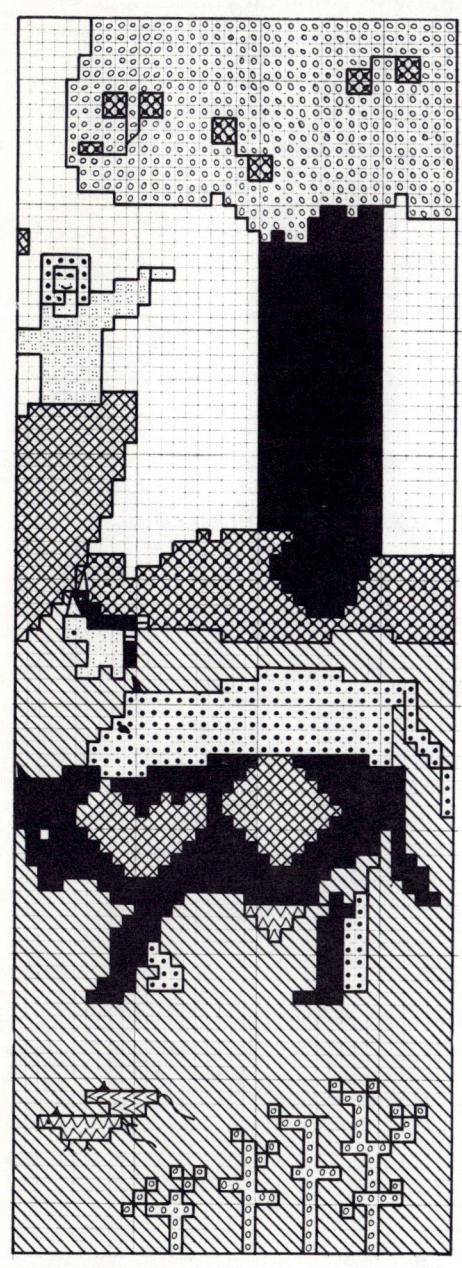

Symbol	Code	Color
⊠	7510	light beige
■	7466	light brown
◨	7341	light green
⊙	7344	green
⊠	7346	dark green
⋁	7293	gray
:	7271	light taupe
⊠	7275	dark taupe
⊟		blanc
·	7170	flesh
⊙	7468	dark brown
◹	7133	pink
⊞	7666	red
⊞	7514	medium brown
◸	7726	light yellow
◿	7436	yellow/orange
∷	7437	buttercup
◿	7301	light blue
☐	7314	sky blue
⊠	7288	dark gray
◩	7439	orange

23

7

Noah's Ark (Pillow)

> But I will establish my Covenant with you, and you must go on board the ark, yourself, your sons, your wife, and your sons' wives, along with you. From all living creatures, from all flesh, you must take two of each kind aboard the ark, to save their lives with yours; they must be a male and a female.
>
> **Genesis 6:18–19.**

SUGGESTED PROJECTS   pillow, framed wall piece, tote bag.

SUGGESTED STITCHES   basket weave or continental, upright cross-stitch, mosaic chain stitch, upright Gobelin; surface embroidery for features and outlines.

ADDITIONAL SUGGESTIONS   For divisions in tree trunk and in frog, use alternating stitches.

8

Ram's Head (Change Purse)

It happened some time later that God put Abraham to the test. "Abraham, Abraham," he called. "Here I am," he replied. "Take your son," God said, "your only child Isaac, whom you love, and go to the land of Moriah. There you shall offer him as a burnt offering, on a mountain I will point out to you."

When they arrived at the place God had pointed out to him, Abraham built an altar there, and arranged the wood. Then he bound his son Isaac and put him on the altar on top of the wood. Abraham stretched out his hand and seized the knife to kill his son.

But the angel of Yahweh called to him from heaven. "Abraham, Abraham," he said. "I am here," he replied. "Do not raise your hand against the boy," the angel said. "Do not harm him, for now I know you fear God. You have not refused me your son, your only son." Then looking up, Abraham saw a ram caught by its horns in a bush. Abraham took the ram and offered it as a burnt offering in place of his son.

Genesis 22:1, 2, 9–13.

SUGGESTED PROJECTS change purse, pincushion, bookmark.

SUGGESTED STITCHES continental or basket weave; surface embroidery for features.

DIRECTIONS FOR MAKING THE CHANGE PURSE

1) After blocking, run several rows of machine stitching around the piece ½ inch from the worked area of the canvas. Trim away the excess canvas.
2) Cut a piece of lining fabric to be used later. This should be ½ inch larger than the piece all around. Suitable fabric is cotton or silk.
3) Fold the piece in half. Steam lightly.
4) With right sides facing, blind-stitch the sides together, leaving room at the top for a zipper.
5) Pin a 4-inch zipper to the top edges. When it is in position, baste it and then sew it with a blind stitch.
6) Fold the lining fabric in half. Sew the sides together using a ½-inch seam allowance. Fold down the top edges by ½ inch. Slip the lining inside the purse and stitch to the top of the canvas.

Graph 8

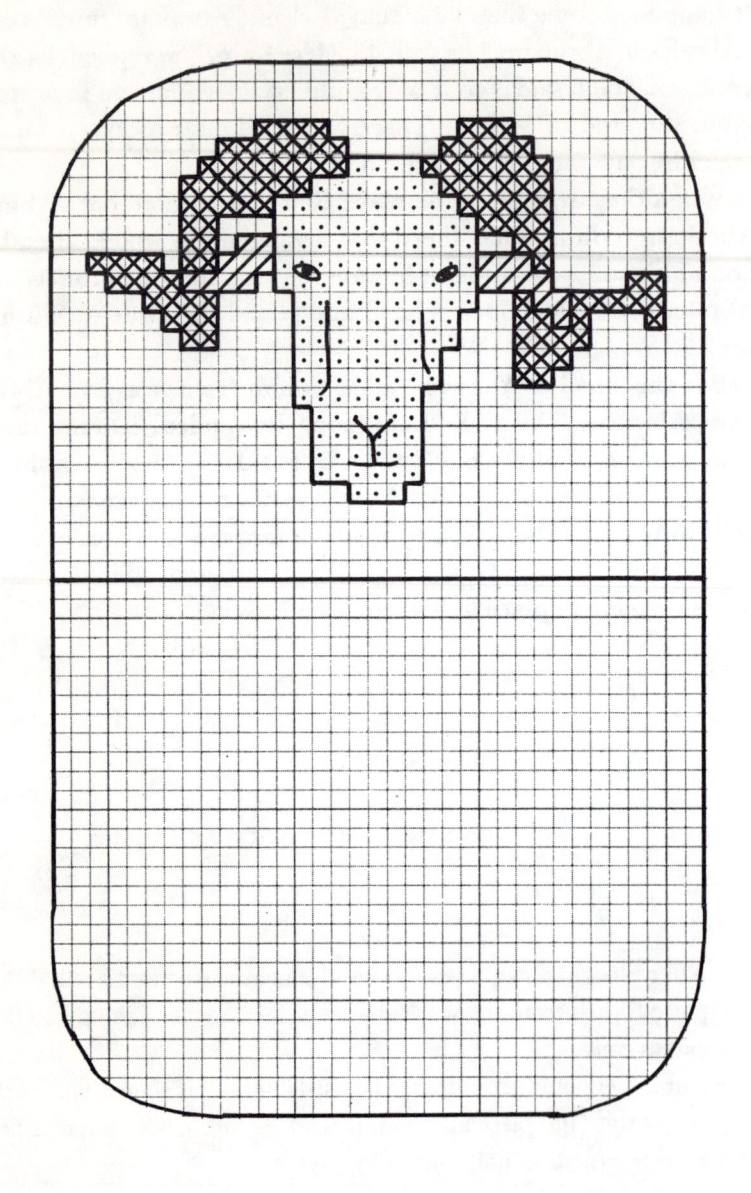

☒ 7518 taupe

◨ 7520 beige

· ecru

☐ 7529 dark brown

9

Abraham (Wall Hanging)

The angel of Yahweh called Abraham a second time from heaven. "I swear by my own self—it is Yahweh who speaks—because you have done this, because you have not refused me your son, your only son, I will shower blessings on you, I will make your descendants as many as the stars of heaven and the grains on the seashore. Your descendants shall gain possession of the gates of their enemies. All the nations of the earth shall bless themselves by your descendants, as a reward for your obedience."

Genesis 22:15–18.

SUGGESTED PROJECTS   wall hanging, pillow, rug.

SUGGESTED STITCHES   continental or basket weave; double cross-stitch for stars, surface embroidery for features.

Graph 9

⊡	7170	flesh
☐	7820	deep purple/blue
■	7423	beige
⊠	blanc	
⊙	7491	light beige
⊟	7715	grey

27

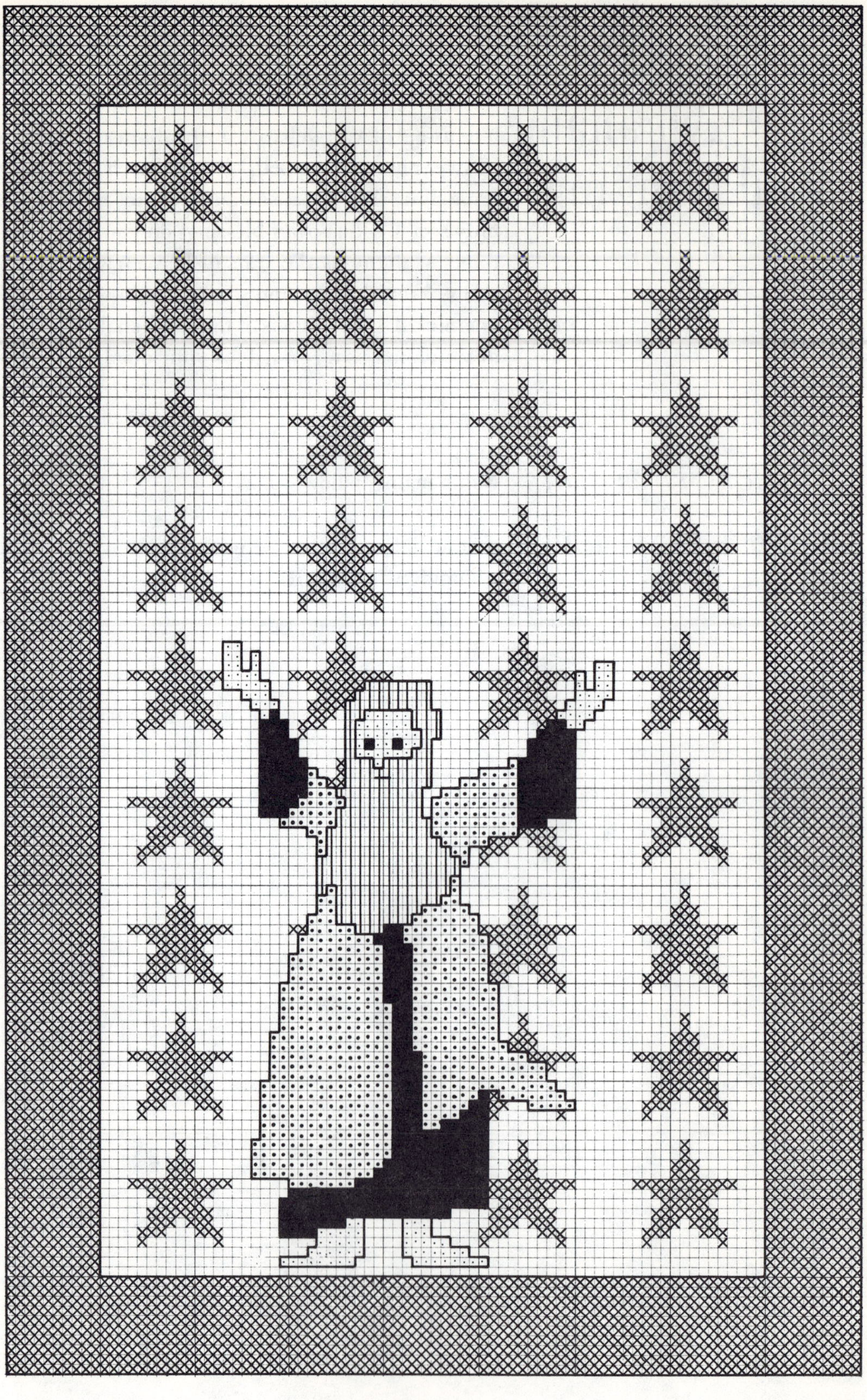

10

Jacob's Ladder (Wall Hanging)

Jacob left Beersheba and set out for Haran. When he had reached a certain place he passed the night there, since the sun had set. Taking one of the stones to be found at that place, he made it his pillow and lay down where he was. He had a dream: a ladder was there, standing on the ground with its top reaching to heaven; and there were angels of God going up it and coming down. And Yahweh was there, standing over him, saying, "I am Yahweh, the God of Abraham your father, and the God of Isaac. I will give to you and your descendants the land on which you are lying. Your descendants shall be like the specks of dust on the ground; you shall spread to the west and the east, to the north and the south, and all the tribes of the earth shall bless themselves by you and your descendants.

Genesis 28:10–24.

SUGGESTED PROJECTS wall hanging.

SUGGESTED STITCHES continental or basket weave, upright cross-stitch, surface embroidery for features.

Graph 10

☐	7307	dark blue	⊙	7786	buttercup
⊠	7500	pale beige	·	7170	flesh
⊘	ecru		■	7928	pale green
⊞	7251	pale pink	⊠	7078	pale yellow
⊡	7960	grey/green			

29

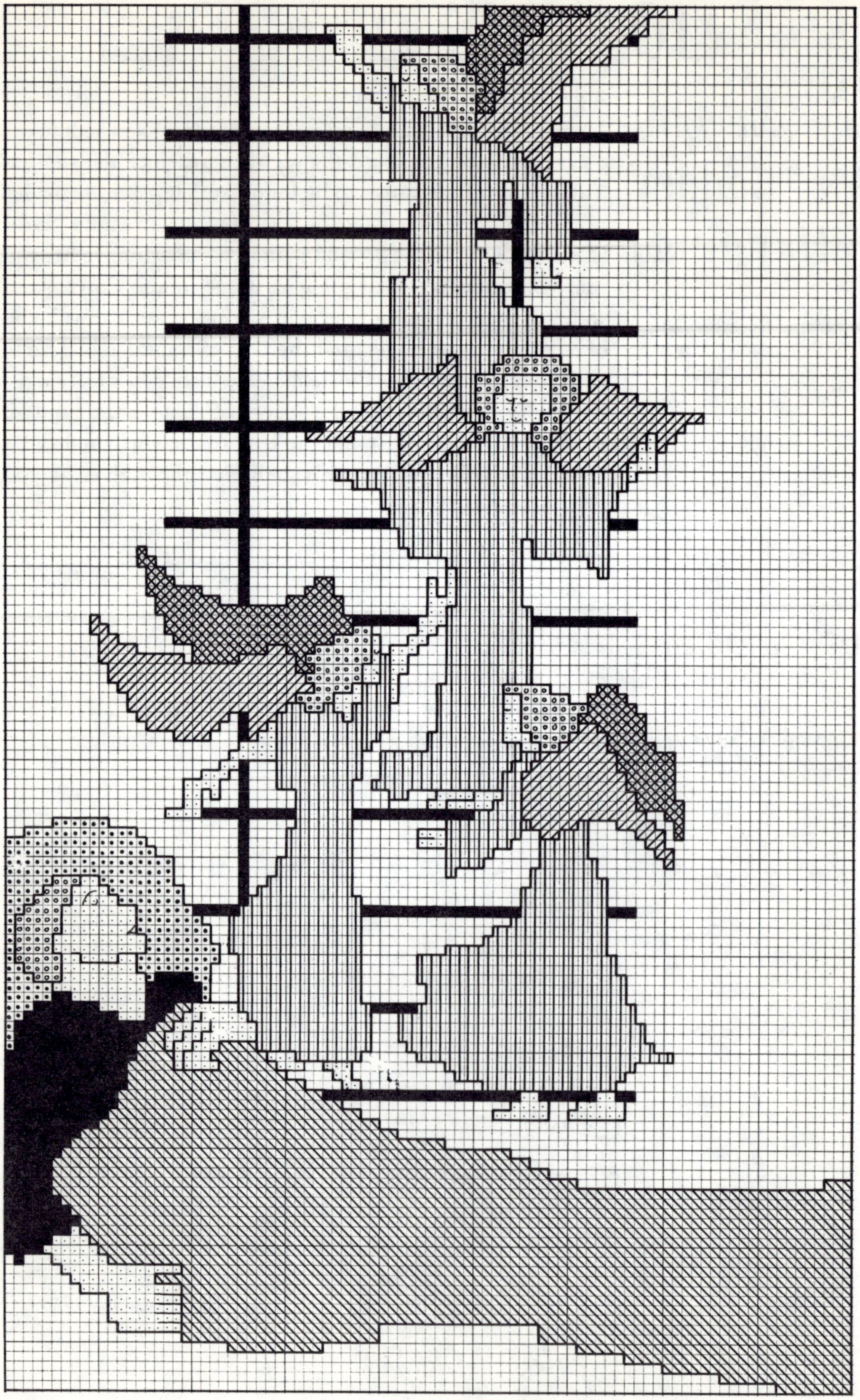

11

Joseph's Dream (Pillow)

Israel loved Joseph more than all his other sons, for he was the son of his old age, and he had a coat with long sleeves made for him. But his brothers, seeing how his father loved him more than all his other sons, came to hate him so much that they could not say a civil word to him.

Now Joseph had a dream, and he repeated it to his brothers, "Listen," he said, "to this dream I have had. We were binding sheaves in the countryside; and my sheaf, it seemed, rose up and stood upright; then I saw your sheaves gather round and bow to my sheaf." "So you want to be king over us," his brothers retorted, "or to lord it over us?" And they hated him still more, on account of his dreams and of what he said. He had another dream which he told to his brothers. "Look, I have had another dream," he said. "I thought I saw the sun, the moon and eleven stars, bowing to me." He told his father and brothers, and his father scolded him. "A fine dream to have!" he said to him. "Are all of us then, myself, your mother and your brothers, to come and bow to the ground before you?" His brothers were jealous of him, but his father kept the thing in mind.

Genesis 37:3–11.

SUGGESTED PROJECTS   needlepoint pillow, wall hanging, cushion cover, footstool cover.

SUGGESTED STITCHES   basket weave, upright cross-stitch, upright Gobelin, mosaic, surface embroidery for the features.

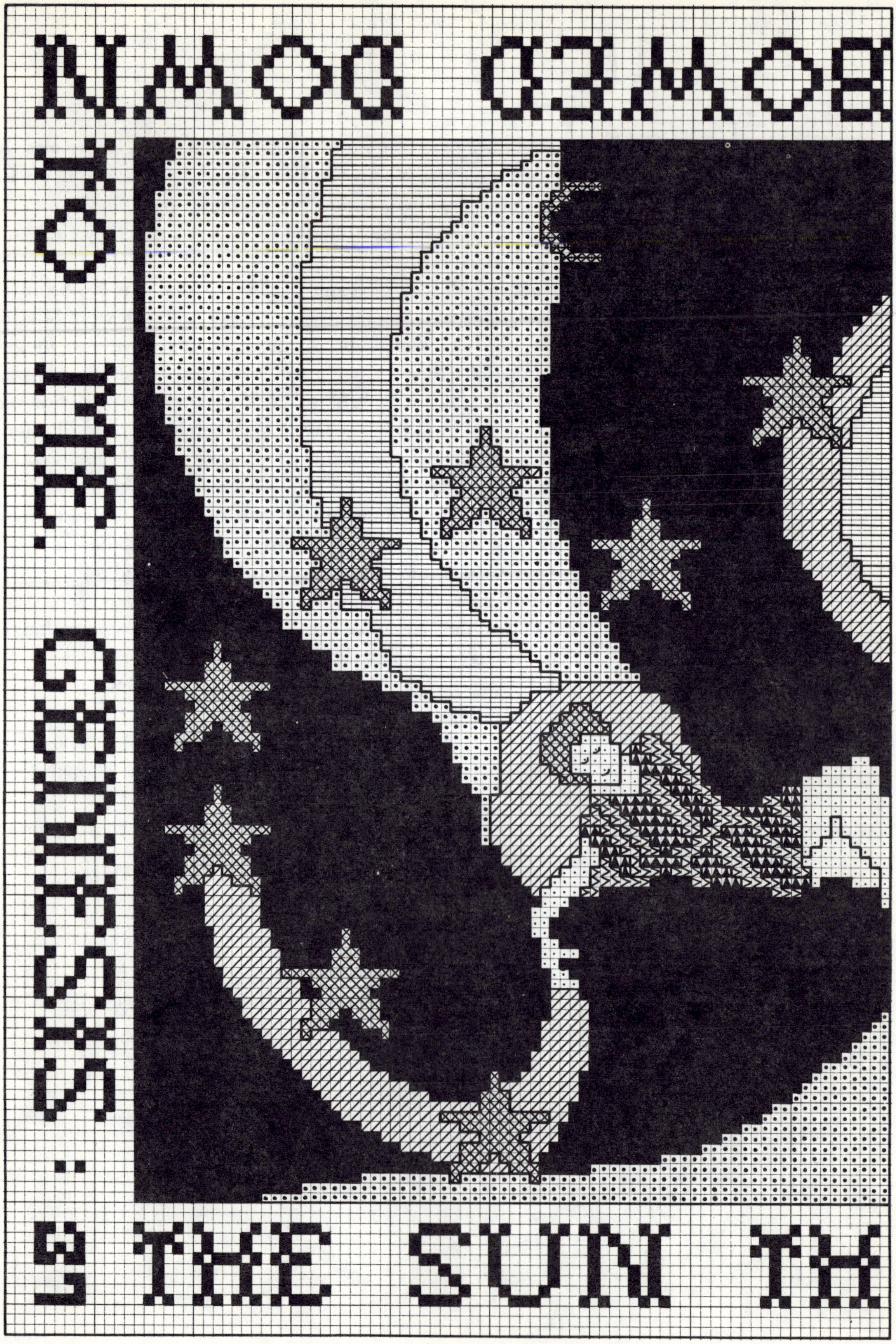
BOWED DOWN
TO ME. GENESIS : 37
THE SUN TH

Graph 11

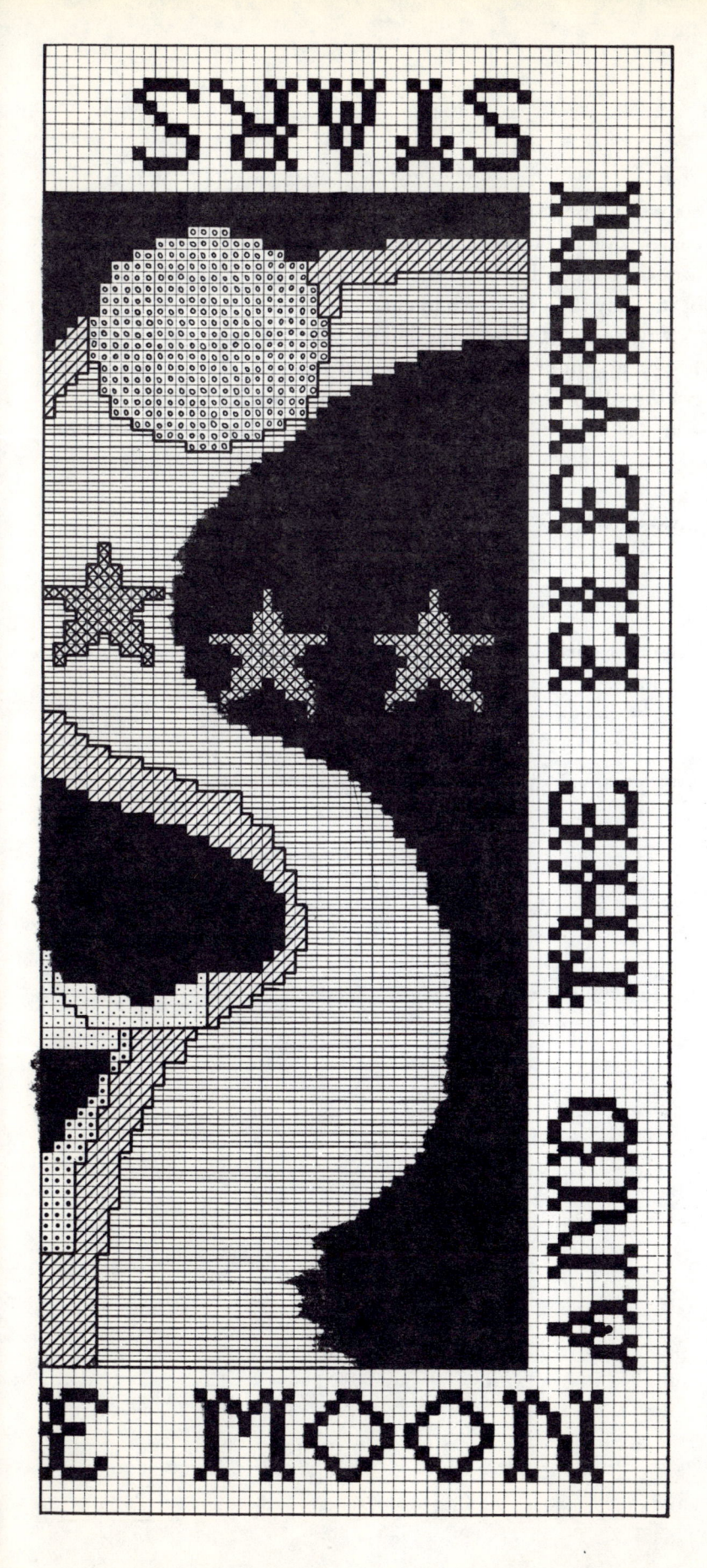

Symbol	Code	Color
■	7317	medium blue
⊠	7745	pale yellow
⊠	7473	mustard
·	7170	flesh
●	7435	bright yellow
╱	7316	light blue
⊙	7314	sky blue
⊟	7313	pale blue
⊳	7771	pale green
▲	7202	light pink
☐	7727	light yellow
⊠	7469	brown

See Color Plate.

12

Camel (Bib)

So, when Joseph reached his brothers, they pulled off his coat, the coat with long sleeves that he was wearing, and catching hold of him they threw him into the well, an empty well with no water in it. They then sat down to eat.

Now some Midianite merchants were passing, and they drew Joseph up out of the well. They sold Joseph to the Ishmaelites for twenty silver pieces, and these men took Joseph to Egypt.

Genesis 37:23–25, 28.

SUGGESTED PROJECTS cross-stitch bib.

ADDITIONAL SUGGESTIONS Use one camel alone for a change purse, pincushion, eyeglass case, bookmark.

SUGGESTED STITCHES cross-stitch, running stitch, French knots.

Graph 12

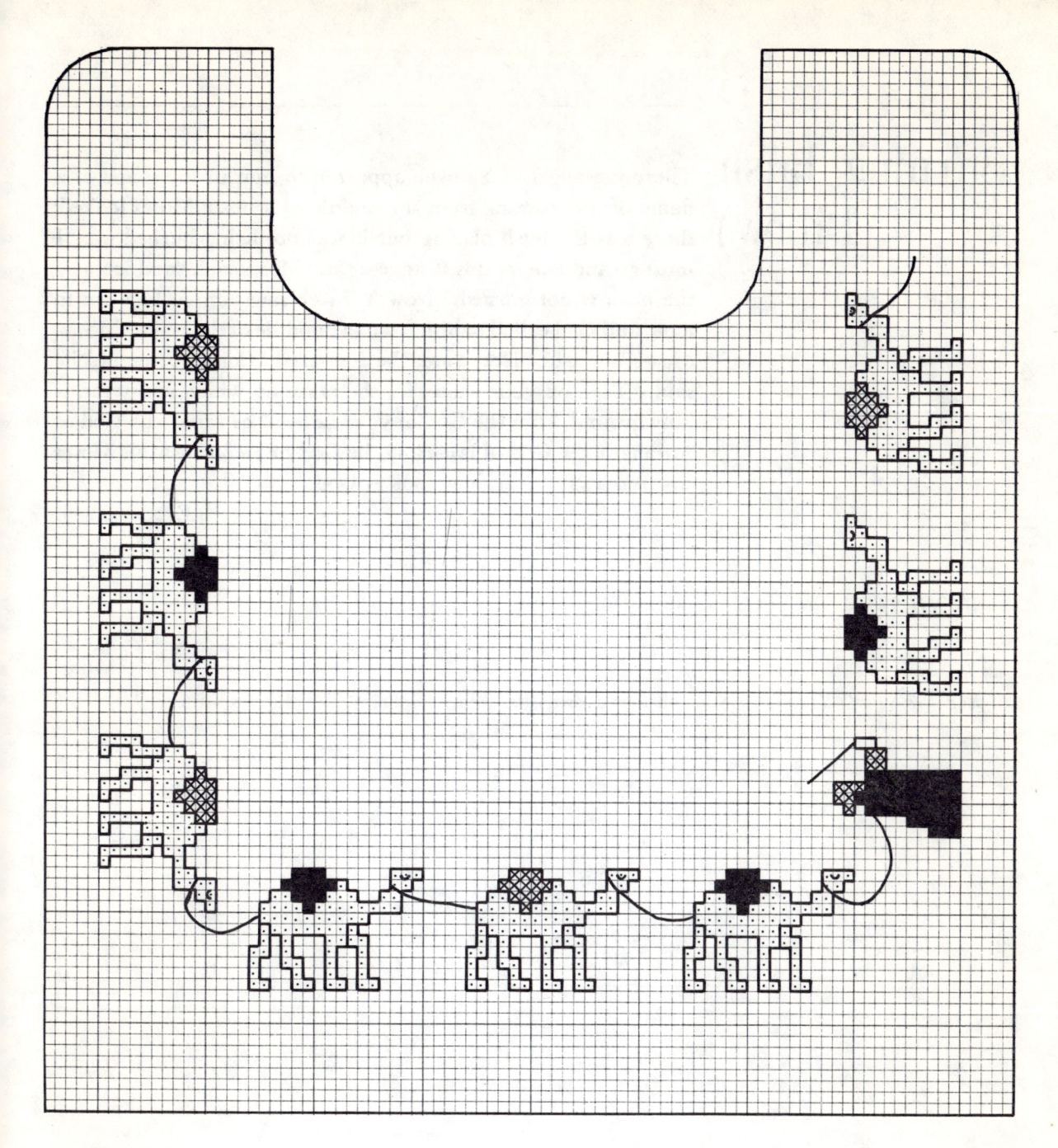

- · 822 beige (DMC perle)
- ■ 309 pink (DMC perle)
- ⊠ 741 gold/yellow (DMC perle)

13

Burning Bush (Pillow)

There the angel of Yahweh appeared to him in the shape of a flame of fire, coming from the middle of a bush. Moses looked; there was the bush blazing but it was not being burned up. "I must go and look at this strange sight," Moses said, "and see why the bush is not burned." Now Yahweh saw him go forward to look, and God called to him from the middle of the bush. "Moses, Moses!" he said. "Here I am," he answered. "Come no nearer," he said. "Take off your shoes, for the place on which you stand is holy ground. I am the God of your father," he said, "the God of Abraham, the God of Isaac and the God of Jacob." At this Moses covered his face, afraid to look at God.

Exodus 3:2–6.

SUGGESTED PROJECTS   pillow, rug.

SUGGESTED STITCHES   continental or basket weave, Gobelin, upright cross-stitch.

Please Note: A ten-square border surrounds this piece.

Graph 13

- ☐ 7255 light magenta
- ⊡ 7434 yellow
- ▽ 7437 orange
- ⊞ 7741 light orange
- ⊠ 7439 deep orange
- ■ 7259 magenta
- ⧄ 7360 rust

37

14

Moses and Ten Commandments (Wall Hanging)

Yahweh said to Moses, "Put these words in writing, for they are the terms of the covenant I am making with you and with Israel."

He stayed there with Yahweh for forty days and forty nights, eating and drinking nothing. He inscribed on the tablets the words of the Covenant—the Ten Words.

When Moses came down from the mountain of Sinai—as he came down from the mountain, Moses had the two tablets of the Testimony in his hands—he did not know that the skin on his face was radiant after speaking with Yahweh. And when Aaron and all the sons of Israel saw Moses, the skin on his face shone so much that they would not venture near him. But Moses called to them, and Aaron with all the leaders of the community came back to him; and he spoke to them. Then all the sons of Israel came closer, and he passed on to them all the orders that Yahweh had given him on the mountain of Sinai.

Exodus 34:27–32.

SUGGESTED PROJECTS — needlepoint wall hanging, pillow.

SUGGESTED STITCHES — continental or basket weave, surface embroidery for features, letters, and outlines.

Graph 14

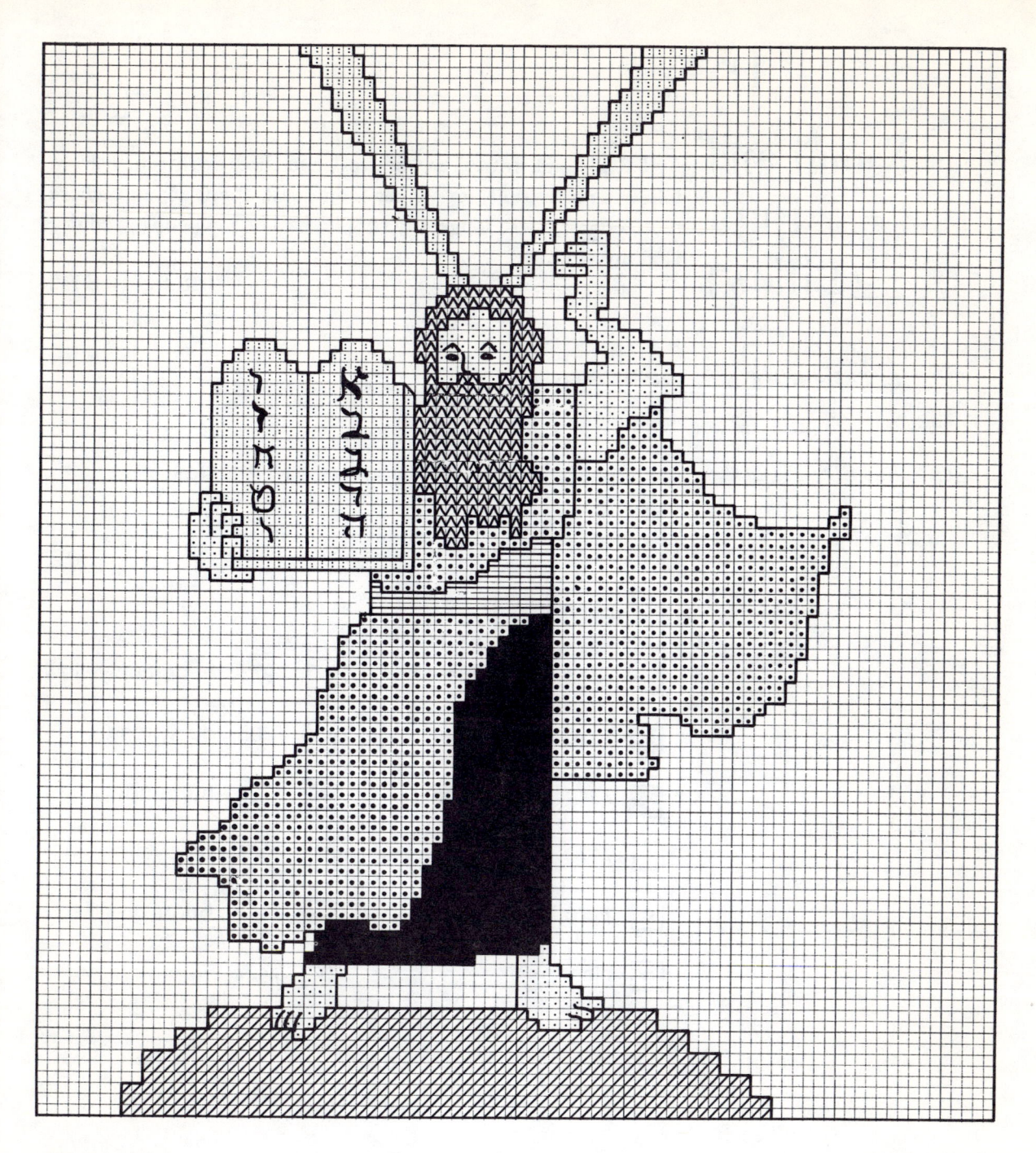

- :·: blanc
- ·•· 7170 flesh
- ⊟ 7245 purple
- ⊡ 7895 light purple
- ■ 7303 rust/orange
- ⊠ 7715 gray
- ⊘ 7798 light blue
- ☐ 7799 medium blue

15

Naomi and Ruth (Pillow)

And Ruth said, Intreat me not to leave thee, or to return from following after thee; for wither thou goest, I will go; and where thou lodgest, I will lodge: thy people shall be my people, and thy God my God.

Ruth I:16 KJV.

SUGGESTED PROJECTS   needlepoint pillow.

SUGGESTED STITCHES   continental or basket weave; surface embroidery for features.

Graph 15

☐	7313	light blue	◪	7973	buttercup yellow
⊠	7316	deep blue	◩	7205	dusty rose
■	7344	light green	⊠	7228	burgundy
⊡	7170	flesh	◨	7905	pale yellow
⊡	7770	medium bright green	⊟	7341	bright green
⊙	blanc		⠿	7544	red

41

16
David with Harp (Pillow)

And it came to pass, when the evil spirit from God was upon Saul, that David took an harp, and played with his hand: so Saul was refreshed, and was well, and the evil spirit departed from him.

I Samuel 16:23 KJV.

SUGGESTED PROJECTS   pillow, framed wall piece, rug.

SUGGESTED STITCHES   basket weave or continental; surface embroidery for features and outlines.

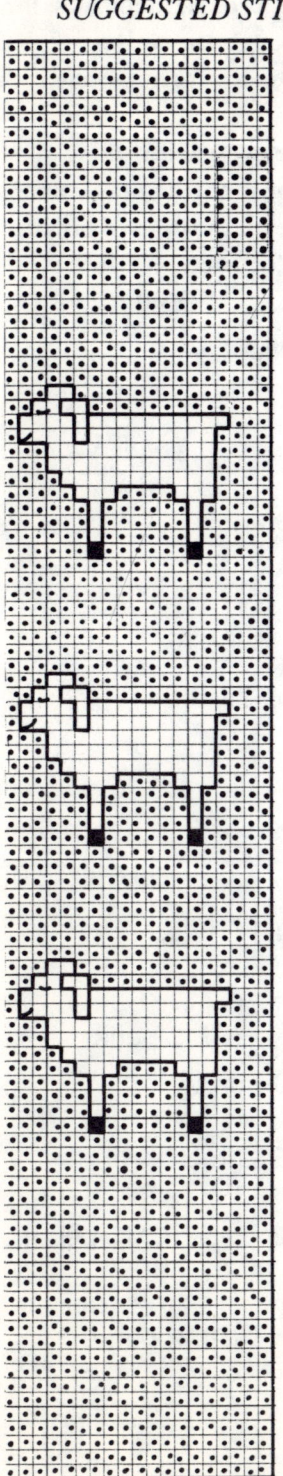

Graph 16

- ⊡ 7170   flesh
- ⊡ 7799   light blue
- ⊘ 7895   purple
- ⊟ 7115   brown
- ⊞ 7820   royal blue
- ⊠ 7342   green
- ■ 310   black (DMC perle)
- ☐ blanc

17

"The Lord Is My Shepherd" (Wall Plaque)

The Lord is my shepherd; I shall not want. He maketh me to lie down in green pastures; he leadeth me beside the still waters. He restoreth my soul: he leadeth me in the paths of righteousness for his name's sake. Yea, though I walk through the valley of the shadow of death, I will fear no evil: for thou art with me; thy rod and thy staff comfort me.

Thou preparest a table before me in the presence of mine enemies: thou anointest my head with oil; my cup runneth over. Surely goodness and mercy shall follow me all the days of my life: and I will dwell in the house of the Lord for ever.

Psalm 23 KJV.

SUGGESTED PROJECTS   cross-stitch plaque.

SUGGESTED STITCHES   cross-stitch, French knots.

Graph 17

Symbol	Code	Color
⋅	712	beige (DMC perle)
:	640	brown (DMC perle)
■	989	green (DMC perle)
╱	312	blue (DMC perle)
⊠	743	yellow (DMC perle)

THE LORD IS
MY SHEPHERD
I SHALL NOT WANT

ABCDEFG
HIJKLMN
OPQRSTU
VWXYZ
12345678
90

46

Graph 18

Symbol	Number	Color
⠂	813	light blue (DMC perle)
⠒	726	yellow (DMC perle)
◪	783	mustard (DMC perle)
◩	826	dark blue (DMC perle)
⊠	900	orange (DMC perle)
■	433	dark brown (DMC perle)
·	700	dark green (DMC perle)
◫	434	light brown (DMC perle)
⊟	953	light green (DMC perle)

See Color Plate.

18

Family Tree (Wall Plaque)

Lo, children are an heritage of the Lord: and the fruit of the womb is his reward.

Psalm 127:3 KJV.

Blessed is every one that feareth the Lord; that walketh in his ways. For thou shall eat the labour of thine hands; happy shalt thou be, and it shall be well with thee. Thy wife shall be as a fruitful vine by the sides of thine house: thy children like olive plants round about thy table. Behold, that thus shall the man be blessed that feareth the Lord. The Lord shall bless thee out of Zion: and thou shalt see the good of Jerusalem all the days of thy life. Yea, thou shalt see thy children's children, and peace upon Israel.

SUGGESTED PROJECTS framed wall plaque.

ADDITIONAL SUGGESTIONS To adapt this to your own family, add leaves if you need additional names; fill in a leaf with cross-stitch where fewer names are needed.

SUGGESTED STITCHES cross-stitch, French knot, running stitch.

19

The Horseman (Rug)

The horse is prepared against the day of battle: but safety is of the Lord.

Proverbs 21:31 KJV.

SUGGESTED PROJECTS   rug, wall banner.

SUGGESTED STITCHES   latch hook or basket weave; surface embroidery for outlines.

Graph 19

☐ 7304   blue

⊡ ecru

⊟ 7520   taupe

◨ gold tinsel

◨ silver tinsel

⊠ 7308   deep purple

⊡ 7170   flesh

⋮ blanc

⊡ 7137   red

■ 7245   purple

49

50

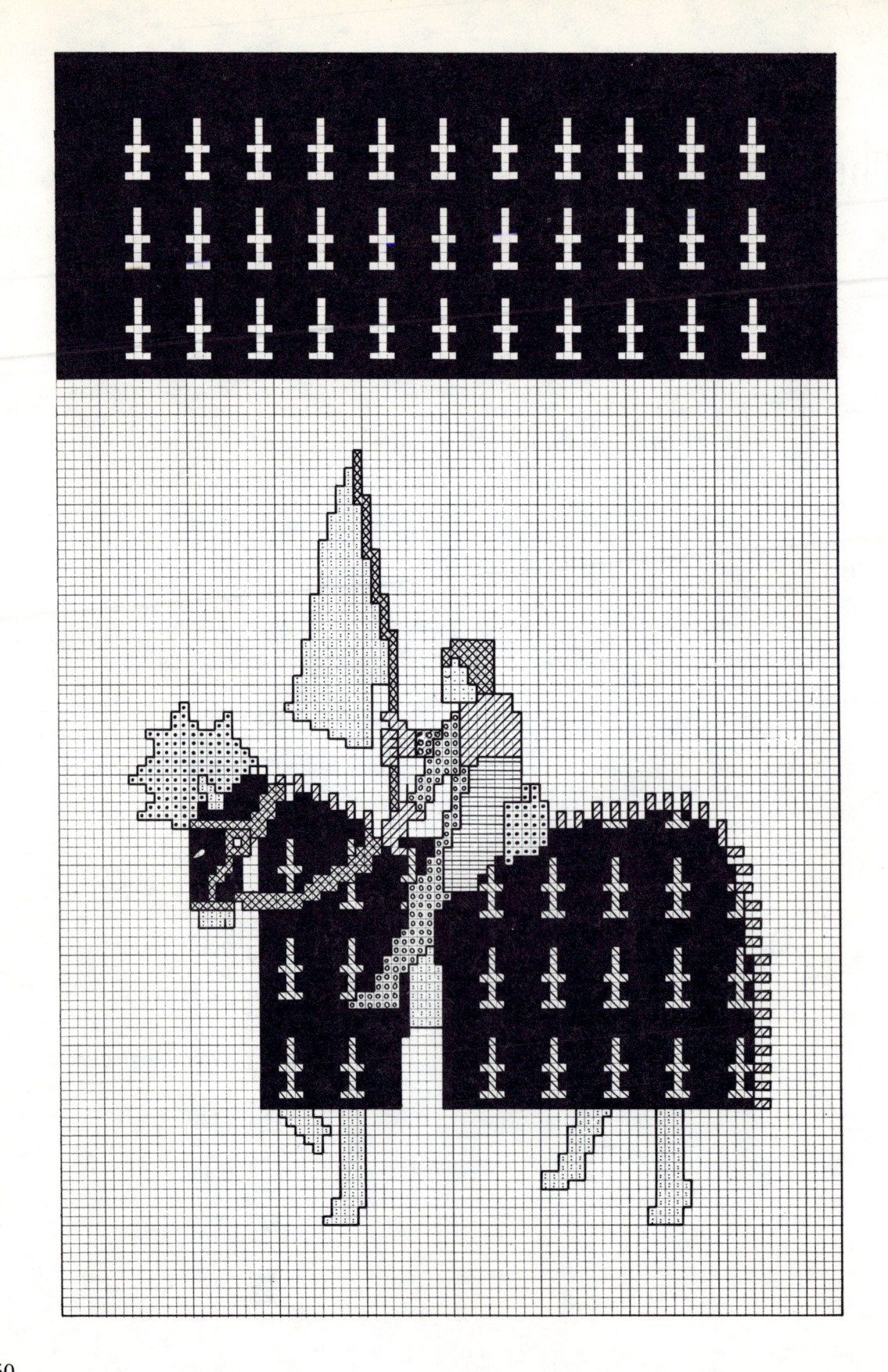

20

Eagle (Wall Hanging)

But they that wait upon the Lord shall renew their strength; they shall mount up with wings as eagles; they shall run, and not be weary; and they shall walk, and not faint.

Isaiah 40:31 KJV.

SUGGESTED PROJECTS wall piece, pillow, tote bag.

SUGGESTED STITCHES basket weave or continental; use alternate stitches to break up patterns on wings and tail feathers; surface embroidery for outlines.

Graph 20

☐	7304	blue	▷ 7266	gray/purple/brown
◪	7845	warm brown	⊡	ecru
◩	7527	medium dark brown	⋮ 7725	yellow
⊠	7999	medium gray/blue	⊙ 7141	light taupe
⊟	7238	light dark brown	⊡ 7339	dark blue/gray
⊟	7742	buttercup	■ 7535	deep dark brown
▽	7529	dark brown		

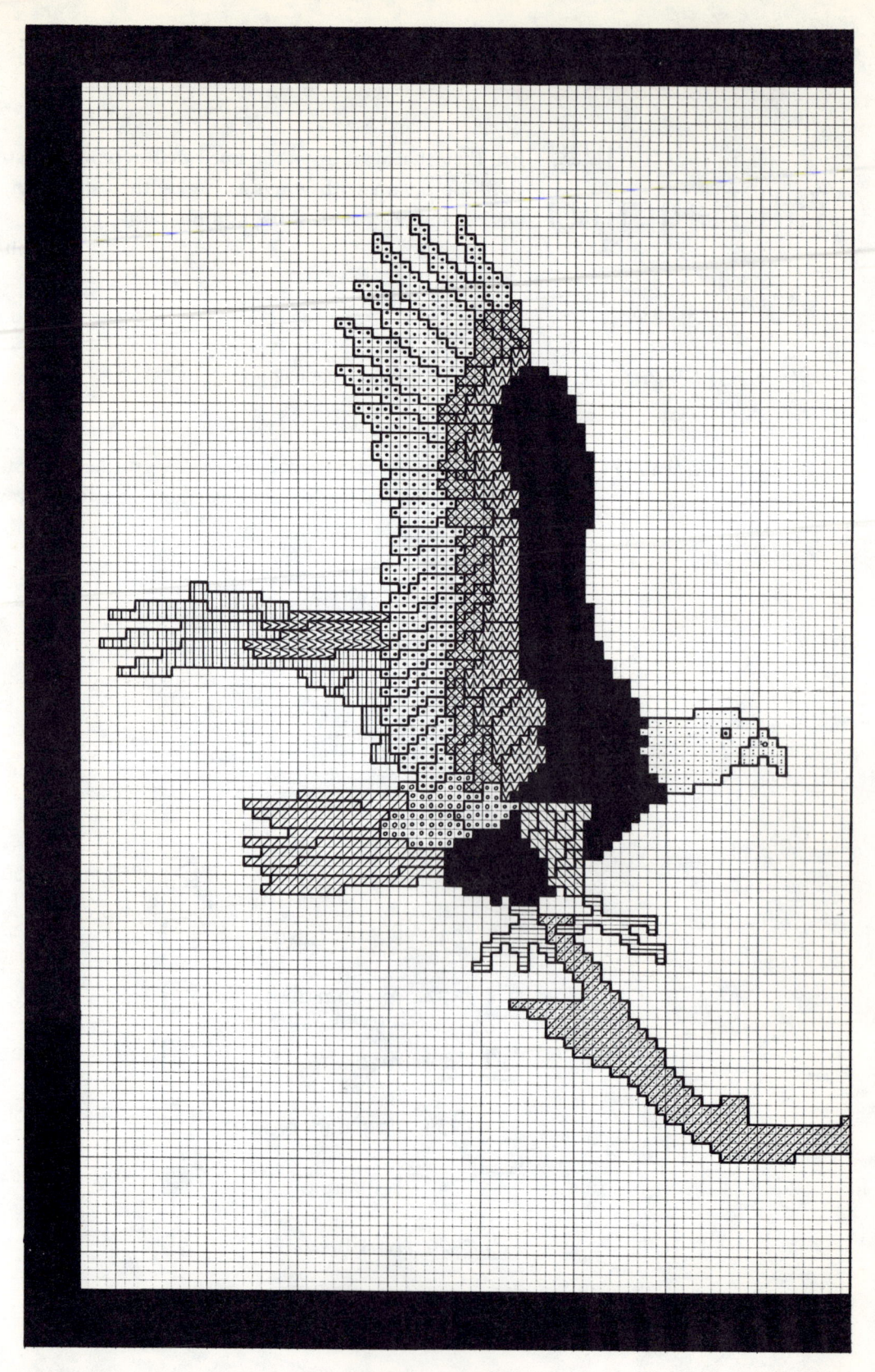

Please Note: A six-square border surrounds this piece.

52

See Graph #5, DOVE EVENING PURSE
Stitched by Dorothy Crosby

See Graph #11, JOSEPH'S DREAM
Stitched by Mary Ann Raph

See Graph #27, WISE MEN ON CAMELS
Stitched by Bano Carlos

See Graph #32, LILIES TOTE BAG
Stitched by Bano Carlos

See Graph #7, NOAH'S ARK
Stitched by Jan Waring

See Graph #18, FAMILY TREE
Stitched by Donna Rothchild

See Graph #38, PENTECOST
Stitched by Jean Covington

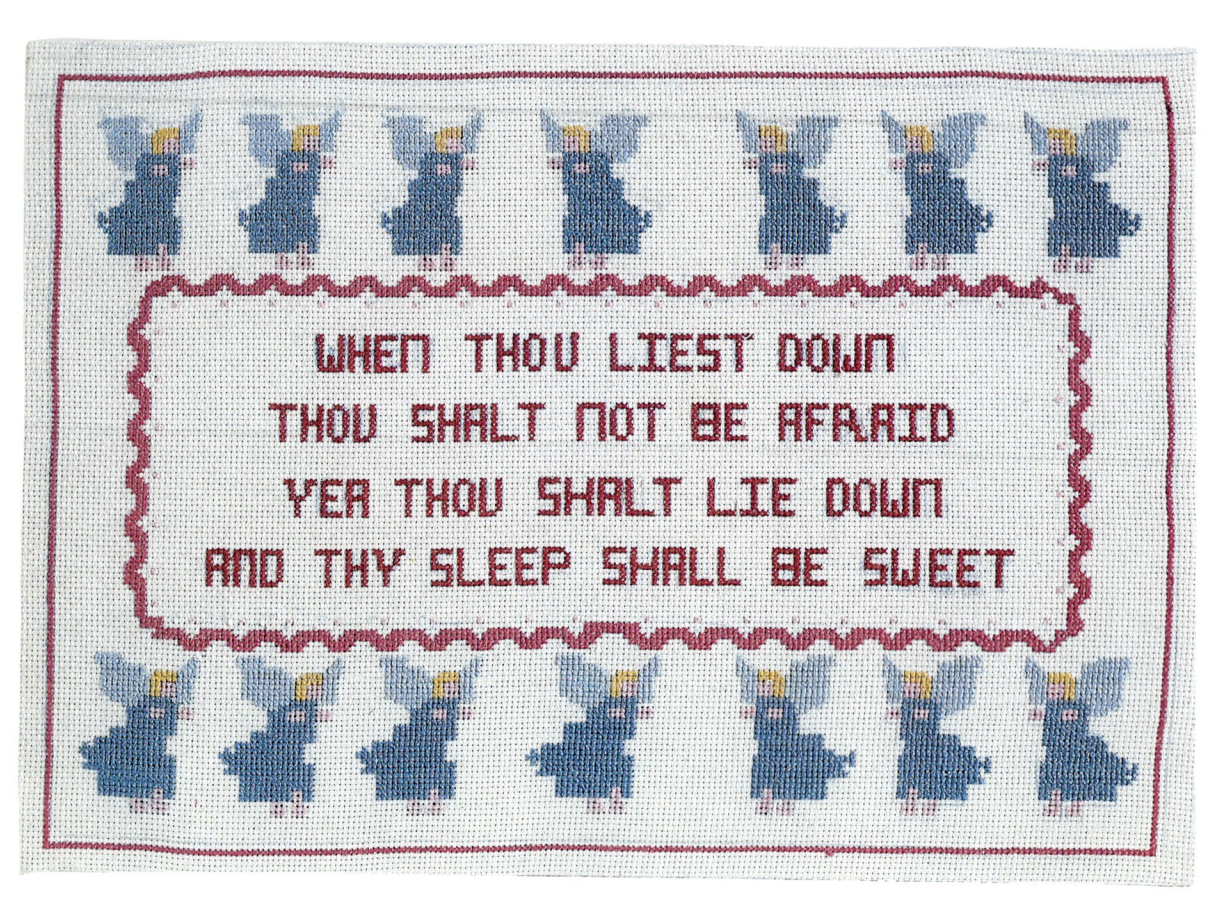

See Graph #40, "WHEN THOU LIEST DOWN"
Stitched by Carole Schwartz

53

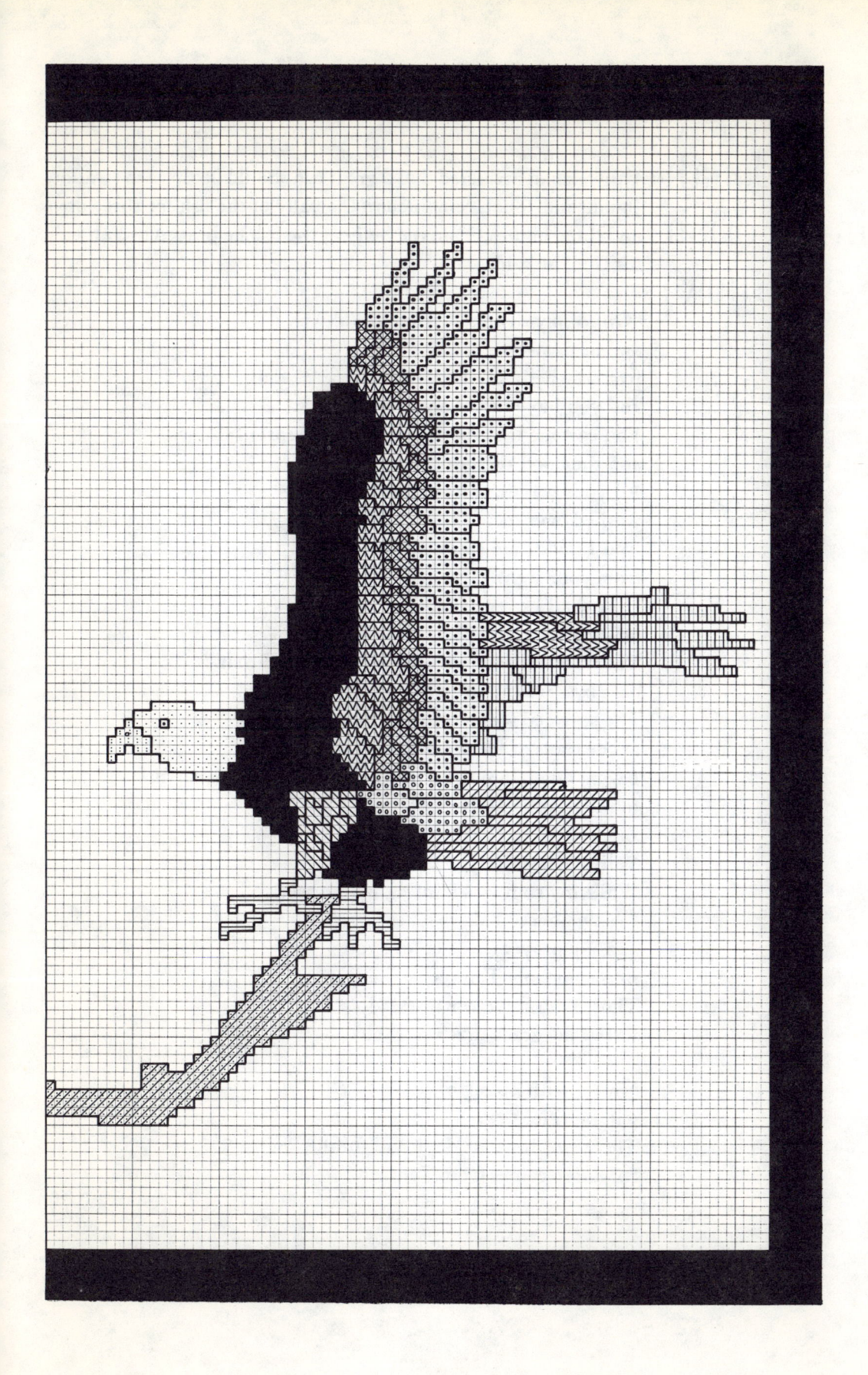

21

Jonah in the Fish (Pillow)

Yahweh had arranged that a great fish should be there to swallow Jonah; and Jonah remained in the belly of the fish for three days and three nights. From the belly of the fish he prayed to Yahweh, his God; he said:

"Out of my distress I cried to Yahweh
and he answered me;
from the belly of Sheol I cried,
and you have heard my voice.
You cast me into the abyss, into the heart of the sea,
and the flood surrounded me.
All your waves, your billows,
washed over me.
And I said: I am cast out
from your sight.
How shall I ever look again
on your holy Temple?
The waters surrounded me right to my throat,
the abyss was all around me.
The seaweed was wrapped around my head
at the roots of the mountains.
I went down into the countries underneath the earth,
to the peoples of the past.
But you lifted my life from the pit,
Yahweh, my God.
While my soul was fainting within me,
I remembered Yahweh,
and my prayer came before you
into your holy Temple.
Those who serve worthless idols
forfeit the grace that was theirs.

"But I, with a song of praise,
will sacrifice to you.
The vow I have made, I will fulfill.
Salvation comes from Yahweh."

Jonah 2:1–10.

SUGGESTED PROJECTS   needlepoint pillow, rug.

ADDITIONAL SUGGESTIONS   Instead of cutting a rectangular border, cut a border to approximate the curves of the fish itself. After construction, this will become a shaped pillow instead of a rectangular one.

SUGGESTED STITCHES   basket weave or continental; surface embroidery for features and outlines.

Graph 21

■ 7820   deep blue

◨ 7137   red

◉ 7786   yellow

⊡ 7155   pink

⊟ 7642   pale sea green

◩ noir

⊡ 7170   flesh

☐ 7737   dark gray

56

57

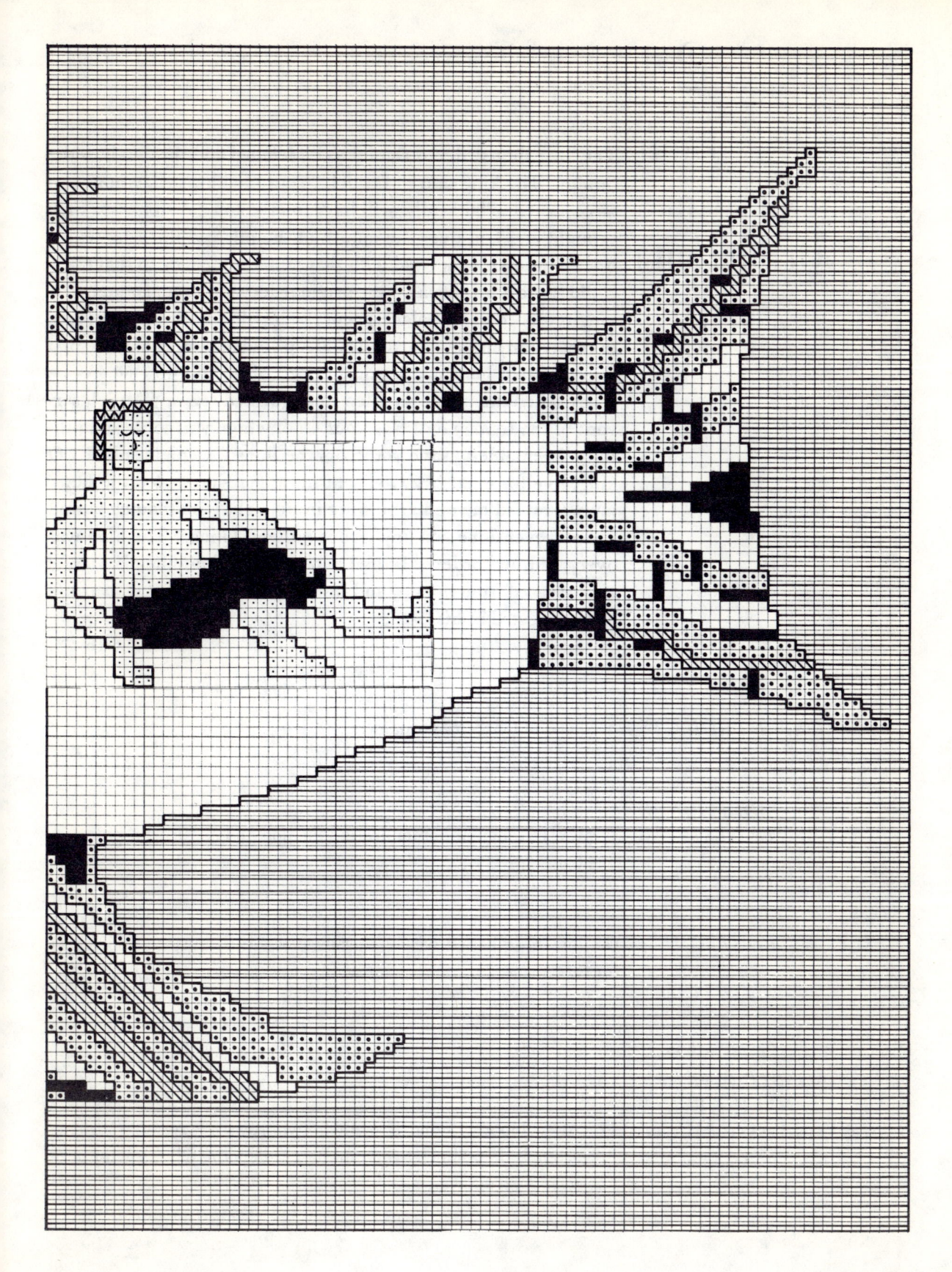

22

Lion (Christmas Ornament)

The king then ordered Daniel to be fetched and thrown into the lion pit. The king said to Daniel, "Your God himself, whom you have served so faithfully, will have to save you." A stone was then brought and laid over the mouth of the pit; and the king sealed it with his own signet and with that of his noblemen, so that there could be no going back on the original decision about Daniel. The king returned to his palace, spent the night in fasting and refused to receive any of his concubines. Sleep eluded him, and at the first sign of dawn he was up, and hurried off to the lion pit. As he approached the pit he shouted in anguished tones, "Daniel, servant of the living God! Has your God, whom you serve so faithfully, been able to save you from the lions?" Daniel replied, "O king, live for ever! My God sent his angel who sealed the lions' jaws, they did me no harm, since in his sight I am blameless, and I have never done you any wrong either, O king." The king was overjoyed, and ordered Daniel to be released from the pit. Daniel was released from the pit, and found to be quite unhurt, because he had trusted in his God.

Daniel 6:16–23.

SUGGESTED PROJECTS needlepoint Christmas ornament.

ADDITIONAL SUGGESTIONS Draw a rectangular border around the lion and construct a pillow or tote bag.

SUGGESTED STITCHES continental or basket weave, upright cross-stitch, surface embroidery for features.

DIRECTIONS FOR CONSTRUCTING A NEEDLEPOINT CHRISTMAS ORNAMENT

1) After blocking, machine-stitch two rows of running stitches around the perimeter close to the needlepoint. Clip, leaving a ½-inch seam allowance.

Graph 22

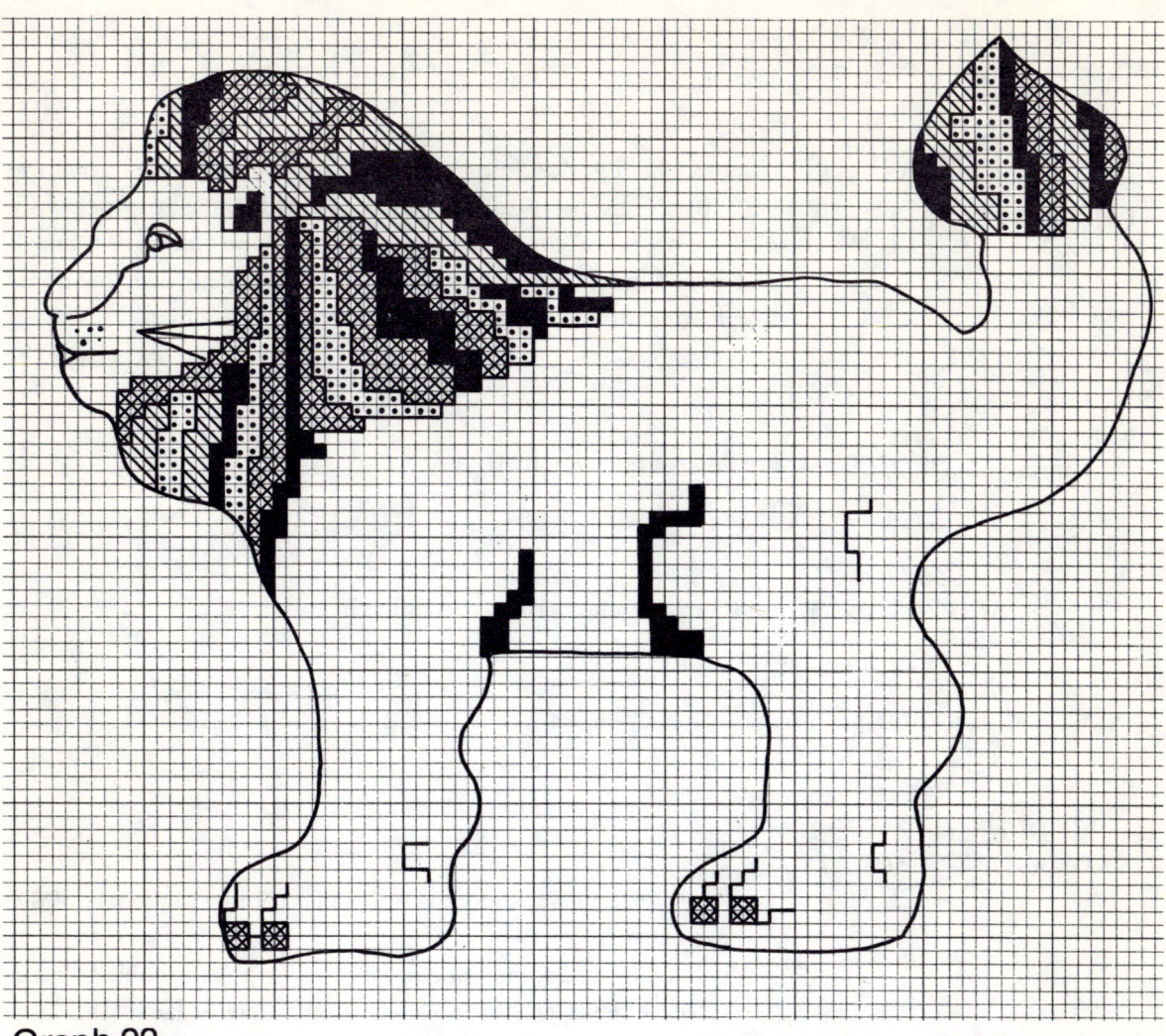

- ☐ 7484 gold
- ⊠ 7496 brown/gold
- ■ 7505 mustard
- ◩ 7444 light rust
- ⊡ 7726 light yellow

2) Cut a piece of velvet or ultrasuede backing.
3) Sew the fabric and the canvas together, right sides facing. Leave a section open for stuffing.
4) Clip corners, turn, stuff.
5) Blind-stitch the opening closed.
6) Attach a ribbon to the top for hanging.

23

Ezekiel's Wheel (Pillow)

> Now as I beheld the living creatures, behold one wheel upon the earth by the living creatures, with his four faces. The appearance of the wheels and their work was like unto the colour of a beryl: and they four had one likeness: and their appearance and their work was as it were a wheel in the middle of a wheel.
>
> Ezekiel 1:15–16 KJV.

SUGGESTED PROJECTS needlepoint pillow, tote, rug.

ADDITIONAL SUGGESTIONS Add a rectangular border for a different shape.

SUGGESTED STITCHES continental or basket weave.

DIRECTIONS FOR CONSTRUCTING A ROUND PILLOW

1) After needlepoint is blocked, stitch bias cording to the face of the needlework.
2) Cut a fabric back the same size as the canvas. A suitable fabric is velvet or velveteen. Stitch bias cording around the face of this also.
3) Cut a length of fabric the circumference of the cushion plus seam allowance.
4) Stitch the two sections of the pillow cover to this strip. Leave an opening. Turn and stuff the pillow.
5) Blind-stitch close the opening.

Graph 23

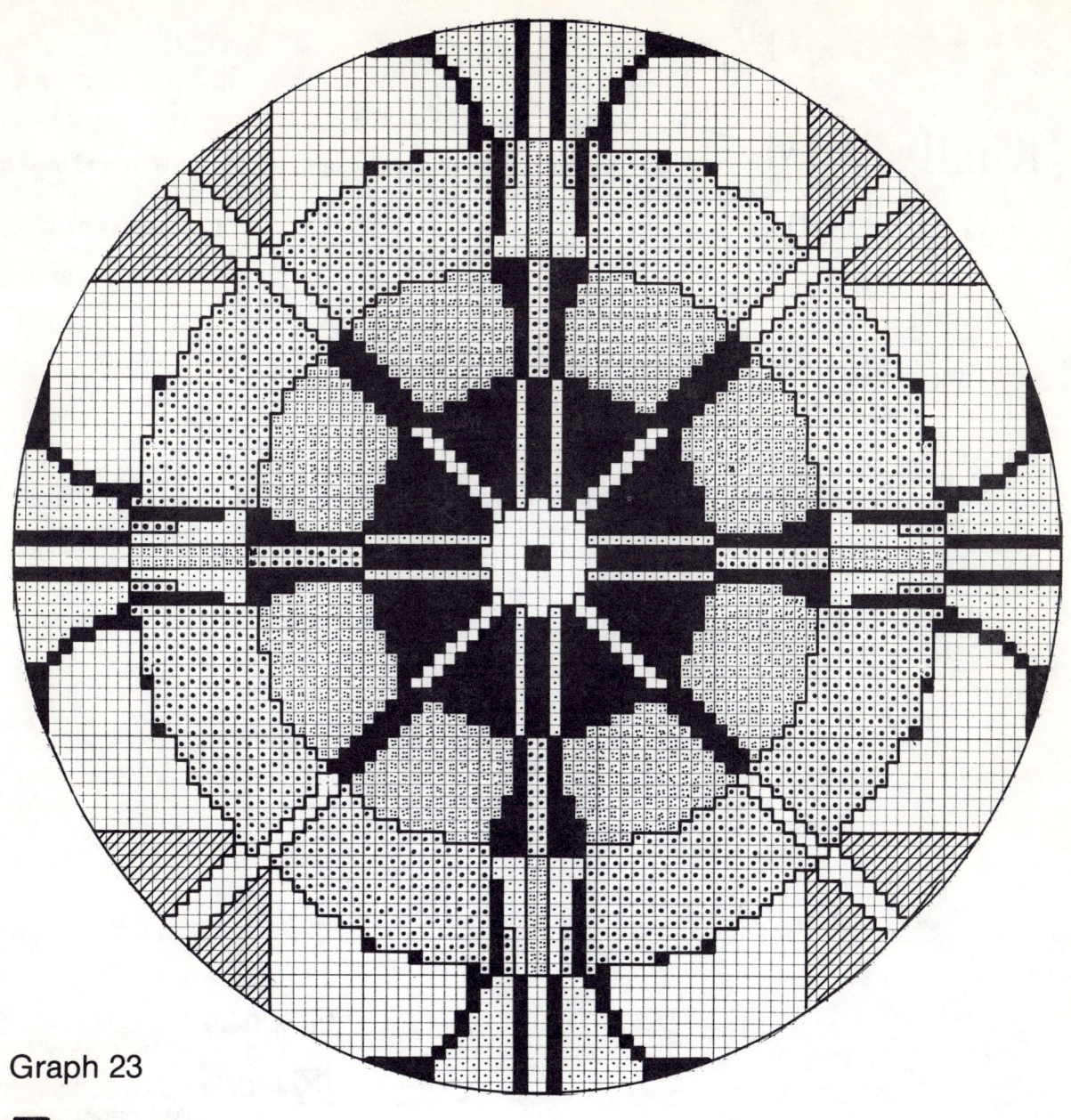

- ■ 7666 red
- ⠋ 7155 bright pink
- ⊡ 7946 deep orange
- ⋅ 7850 medium orange
- ◪ 7153 light pink
- □ 7852 pale orange

24

"Kindly Words" (Wall Plaque)

Pleasant words are as an honeycomb, sweet to the soul, and health to the bones.

Proverbs 16:24 KJV.

SUGGESTED PROJECTS   wall plaque.

ADDITIONAL SUGGESTIONS   The bee can be isolated as a design motif and translated into needlepoint. Then use it in a pincushion, a bookmark, or a change purse.

SUGGESTED STITCHES   cross-stitch.

Graph 24

Symbol	Code	Color
⊠	989	green (DMC perle)
⊡	743	light yellow (DMC perle)
·	740	medium yellow (DMC perle)
■	301	brown (DMC perle)
⧄	402	brown (DMC perle)

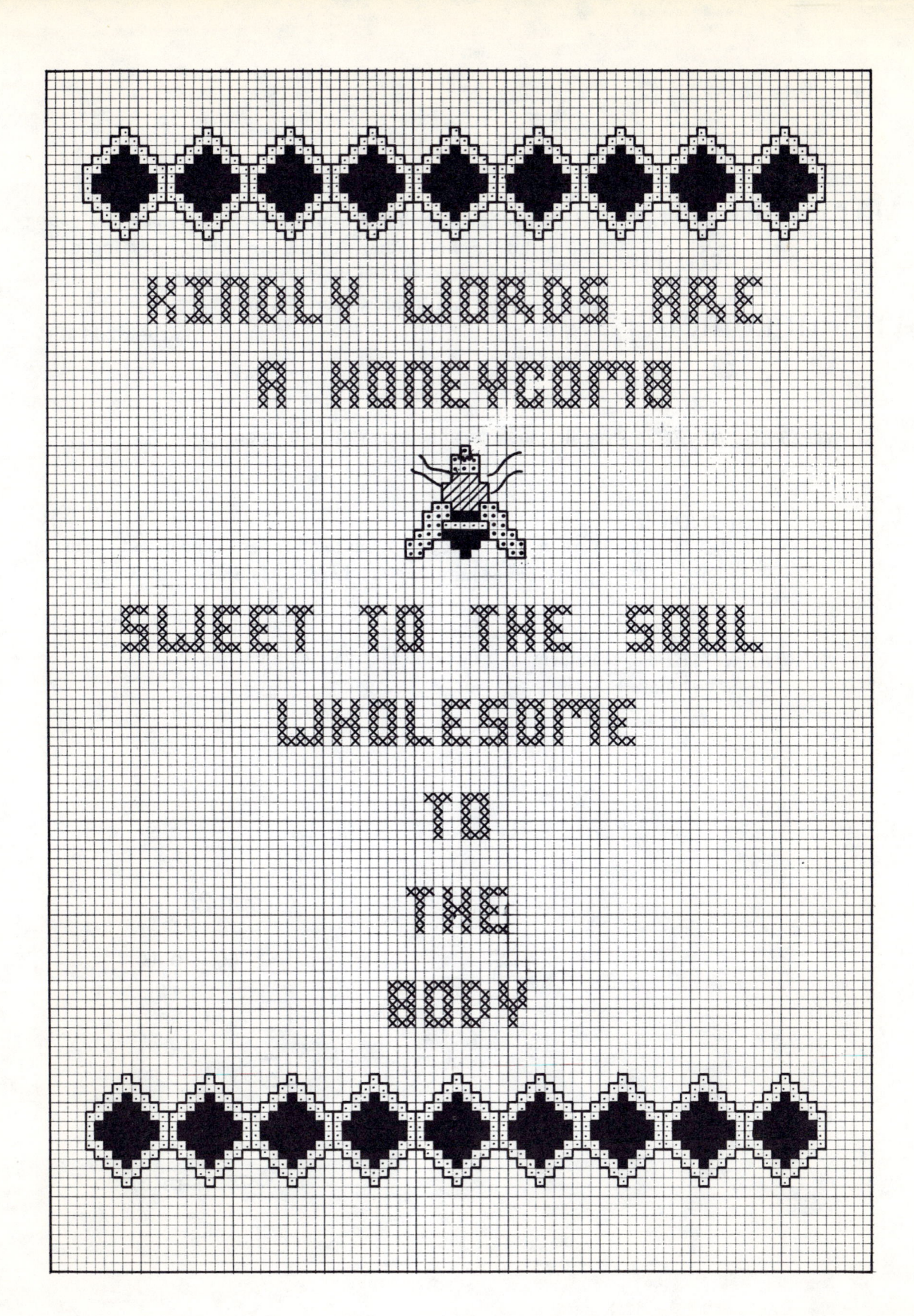

KINDLY WORDS ARE
A HONEYCOMB

SWEET TO THE SOUL

WHOLESOME

TO

THE

BODY

25

Mary and Baby (Birth Announcement)

And when they were come into the house, they saw the young child with Mary his mother, and fell down, and worshipped him: and when they had opened their treasures, they presented unto him gifts; gold, and frankincense, and myrrh.

Matthew 2:11 KJV.

SUGGESTED PROJECTS needlepoint birth announcement, wall plaque, pillow.

ADDITIONAL SUGGESTIONS Work in cross-stitch; adapt this to other names and dates by using the alphabet in the sampler "The Lord Is My Shepherd." (Graph #17)

SUGGESTED STITCHES continental; surface embroidery for outlines.

Graph 25

Symbol	Code	Color
⊠	7605	pink (or, 7313, blue)
▫	7170	flesh
◨	7434	yellow
⊡	7341	green
◪	7800	pale blue
☐		blanc

65

26

Star (Christmas Ornament)

Praise ye the Lord. Praise ye the Lord from the heavens: praise him in the heights. Praise ye him, all his angels: praise ye him, all his hosts. Praise ye him, sun and moon: praise him all ye stars of light. Praise him, ye heavens of heavens, and ye waters that be above the heavens. Let them praise the name of the Lord: for he commanded, and they were created.

Psalm 148:1–5 KJV.

SUGGESTED PROJECTS needlepoint Christmas ornament.

ADDITIONAL SUGGESTIONS Add a rectangular border around the design and construct as a pillow, tote bag, chair cushion.

SUGGESTED STITCHES continental or basket weave.

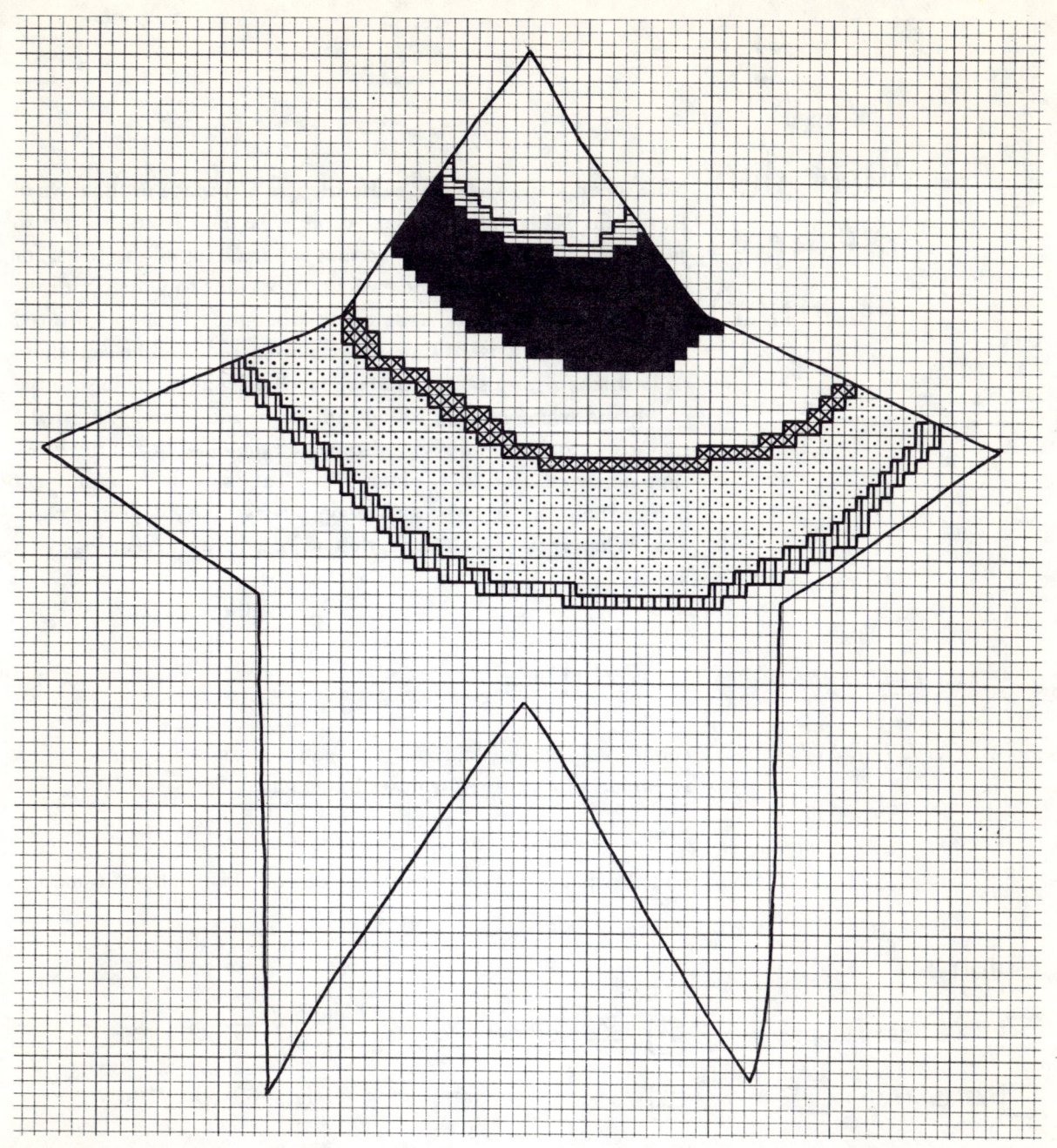

For directions to make a Christmas ornament, see LION Christmas ornament, Graph #22.

Graph 26

- ☐ 7995 robin's egg blue
- ■ 7155 bright pink
- ⊟ 7434 bright yellow
- · 7435 buttercup
- ⊠ gold tinsel
- ⊡ silver tinsel

27

Wise Men on Camels (Banner)

Now when Jesus was born in Bethlehem of Judaea in the days of Herod the King, behold, there came wise men from the east to Jerusalem, Saying, Where is he that is born King of the Jews? for we have seen his star in the east, and are come to worship him.

Then Herod, when he had privily called the wise men, inquired of them diligently what time the star appeared. And he sent them to Bethlehem, and said, Go and search diligently for the young child; and when ye have found him, bring me word again, that I may come and worship him also. When they had heard the king, they departed, and, lo, the star, which they saw in the east, went before them, till it came and stood over where the young child was. When they saw the star, they rejoiced with exceeding great joy.

Matthew 2:1–2, 7–10 KJV.

SUGGESTED PROJECTS   needlepoint banner.

SUGGESTED STITCHES   continental, mosaic, upright cross-stitch, upright Gobelin; surface embroidery for textures, features, and outlines.

ADDITIONAL SUGGESTIONS   Use alternating stitches to create patterns on tree trunk and camels.

Graph 27

Symbol	Code	Color	Symbol	Code	Color	Symbol	Code	Color
⊠	7466	deep taupe	⊙	7666	orange/red	◻	7139	dark red
⊡	7170	flesh	⊟	7342	bright green	⋰	7469	dark brown
■		gold tinsel	⋁	7243	light purple	⊠	7255	light burgundy
⊠	7259	burgundy	:	7155	pink	⊘	7253	pale old rose
⊠	7245	deep purple	⊓	7544	dull red	☐	7251	pale lilac
⊙	7467	brown	⊠	7820	deep blue	▷	7463	light brown
⟋	7137	red	⊞	7137	maroon/red	⊘	7769	dull green

68

See Color Plate.

28

King (Christmas Ornament)

> It is the glory of God to conceal a thing: but the honour of kings is to search out a matter.
>
> Proverbs 25:2 KJV.

SUGGESTED PROJECTS   needlepoint Christmas ornament.

ADDITIONAL SUGGESTIONS   Add a rectangular border around the design and construct as a pillow, tote bag, chair cushion.

SUGGESTED STITCHES   continental or basket weave; surface embroidery for features.

Graph 28

- ☐ 7170 flesh
- ⊡ gold tinsel
- ⊡ 7435 bright yellow
- ■ 7341 bright green
- ◩ 7708 deep lilac
- ◪ 7245 purple

For directions to make a Christmas ornament, see LION Christmas ornament, Graph #22.

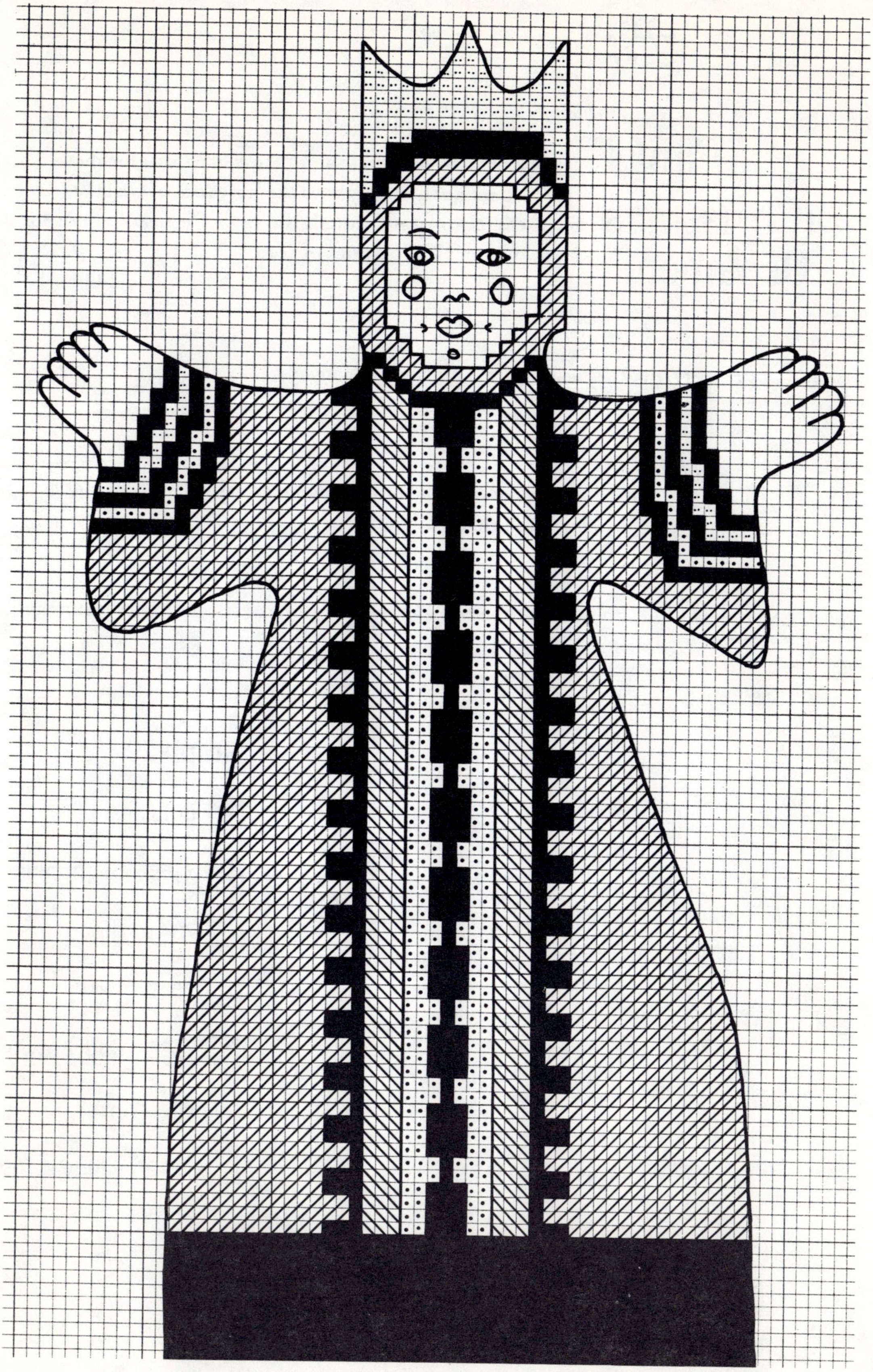

29

Camel (Christmas Ornament)

Jesus looked at him and said, "How hard it is for those who have riches to make their way into the kingdom of God! Yes, it is easier for a camel to pass through the eye of a needle than for a rich man to enter the kingdom of God."

Luke 18:24–25.

SUGGESTED PROJECTS needlepoint Christmas ornament.

ADDITIONAL SUGGESTIONS Add a rectangular border around the design and construct as a pillow, tote bag, chair cushion.

SUGGESTED STITCHES continental or basket weave; surface embroidery for features.

Graph 29

Symbol	Code	Color
■		gold tinsel
⊠	7155	bright pink
⊘	7342	green
⊙	7640	red
◨	7526	dark brown
⋅		silver tinsel
□	7512	sandy beige

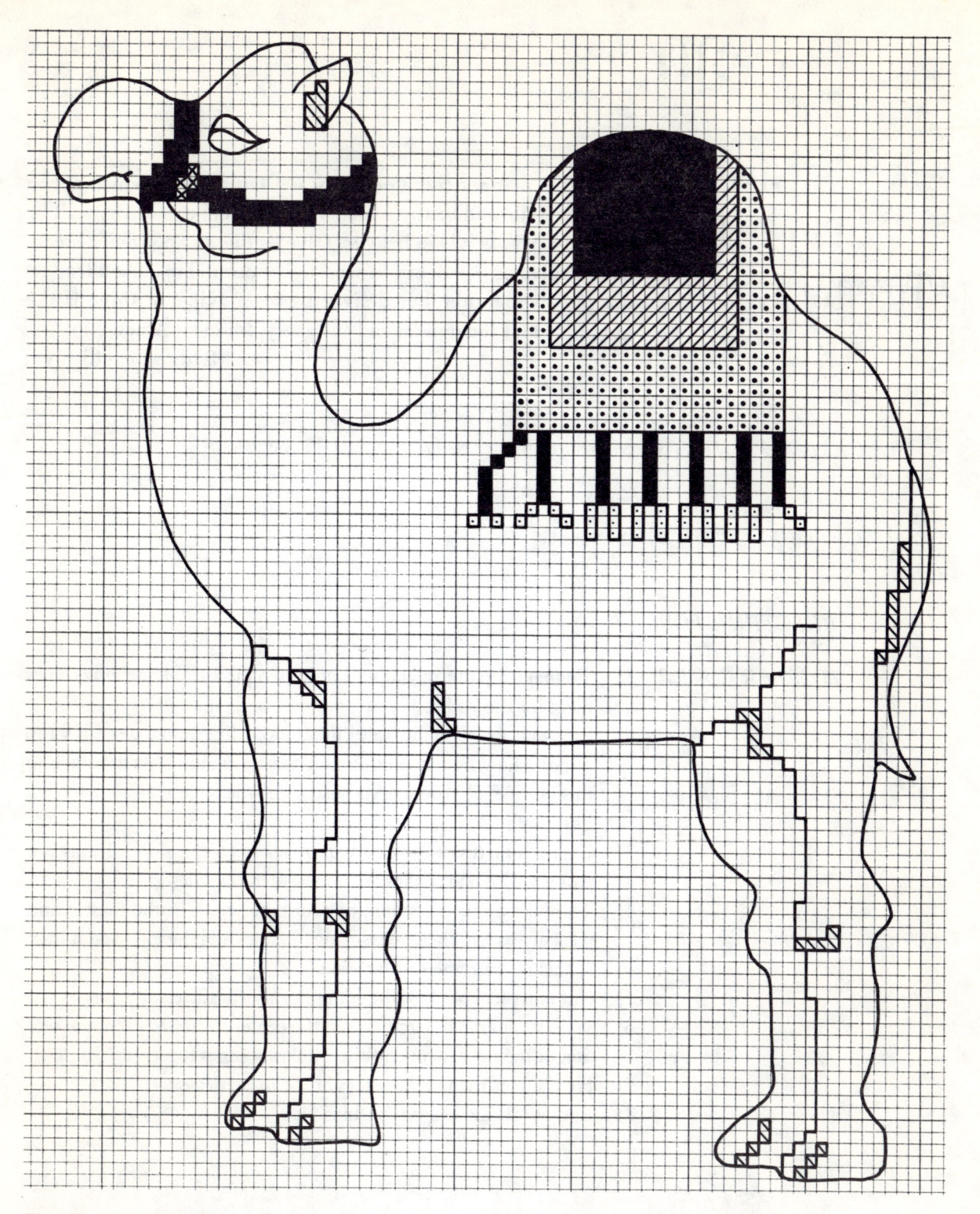

For directions to make a Christmas ornament, see LION Christmas ornament, Graph #22.

30

"Give Us This Day" (Toaster Cover)

After this manner therefore pray ye: Our Father which art in heaven, Hallowed be thy name. Thy kingdom come. Thy will be done in earth, as it is in heaven. Give us this day our daily bread. And forgive us our debts, as we forgive our debtors. And lead us not into temptation, but deliver us from evil: For thine is the kingdom, and the power, and the glory, for ever. Amen.

Matthew 6:9–13 KJV.

SUGGESTED PROJECTS   cross-stitch toaster cover, tea towel, kitchen cloth.

SUGGESTED STITCHES   cross-stitch.

DIRECTIONS FOR CONSTRUCTING A TOASTER COVER

1) To make a pattern, you will need two pieces and one long center piece for the width of your toaster.
2) Lay your toaster on its side. Trace its outline onto a piece of scrap paper, allowing for extension of toaster handles. Add ½ inch to this outline all around. And use your tracing line as your sewing line.
3) Cut two pieces of aida or hardanger linen the same size as the pattern. Use one of these to cross-stitch your design.
4) To make a center section, measure the width of the toaster and measure its length by measuring the sides and the top. Add ½ inch to this measurement all around.
5) Cut one piece of cloth the same size as the pattern.
6) With wrong sides together, pin the center section to each side section of the toaster cover. Stitch the raw edges together.
7) Hem under the bottom edges of the toaster cover.
8) Encase all raw edges with bias tape.

Graph 30

- ⊡ 301 warm brown
  (DMC perle)
- ■ 743 golden yellow
  (DMC perle)
- ⊠ 740 orange/yellow
  (DMC perle)
- ⌺ 989 green
  (DMC perle)
- ⊟ 822 beige
  (DMC perle)

31

The Good Shepherd (Wall Plaque)

"What man among you with a hundred sheep, losing one, would not leave the ninety-nine in the wilderness and go after the missing one till he found it? And when he found it, would he not joyfully take it on his shoulders and then, when he got home, call together his friends and neighbors? "Rejoice with me," he would say, "I have found my sheep that was lost." In the same way, I tell you, there will be more rejoicing in heaven over one repentant sinner than over ninety-nine virtuous men who have no need of repentance.

Luke 15:4–7.

SUGGESTED PROJECTS   needlepoint wall plaque, pillow.

SUGGESTED STITCHES   basket weave; surface embroidery for stitches.

Graph 31

Symbol	Code	Color
☐	blanc	
◩	7344	grass green
⊠	7342	green
⊟	7340	light green
⊡	7421	light brown
⊙	7515	dark brown
■	7666	red
◨	7313	sky blue
⊡	7301	light blue
◪	7307	dark blue
⊡	7170	flesh

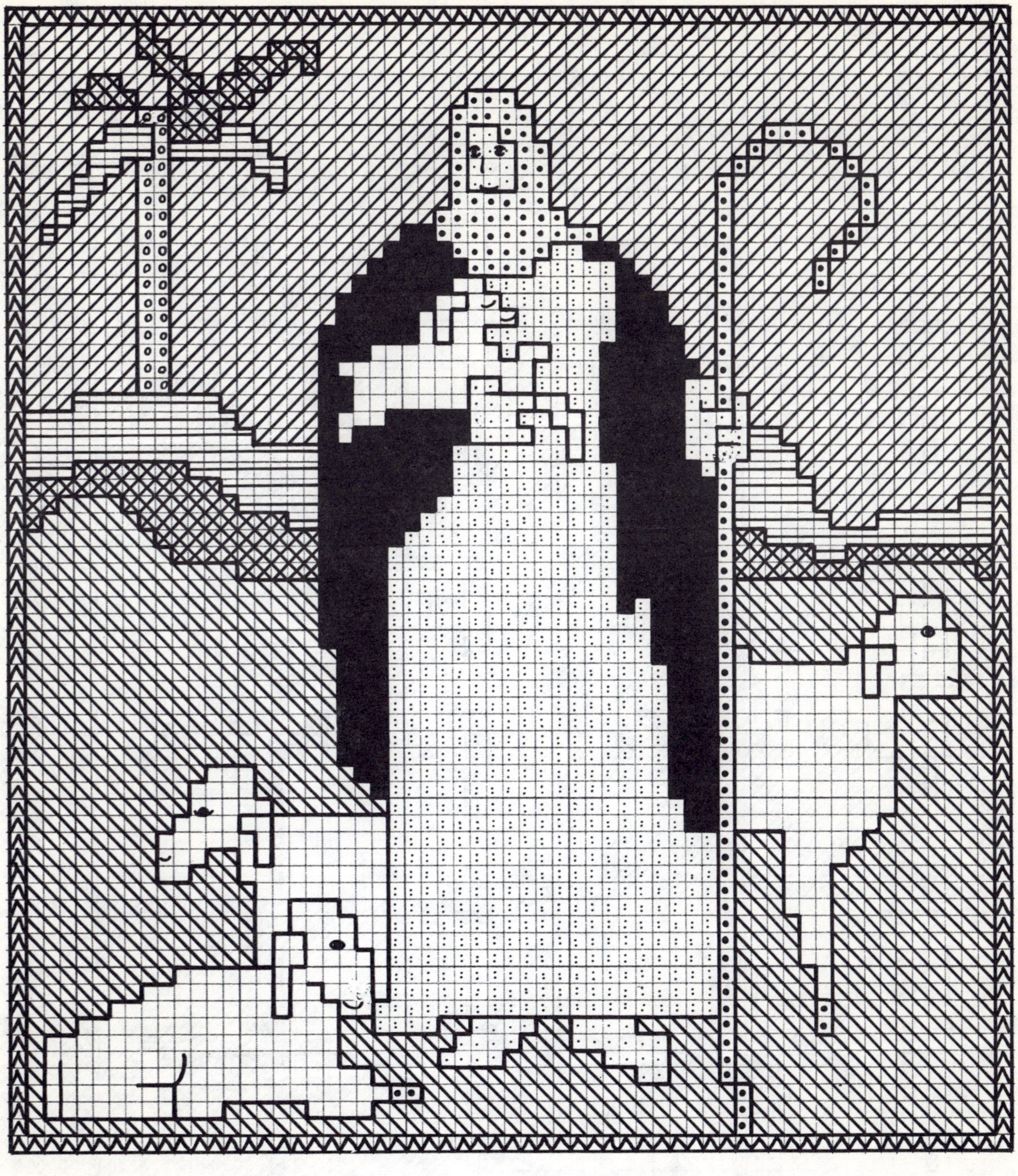

78

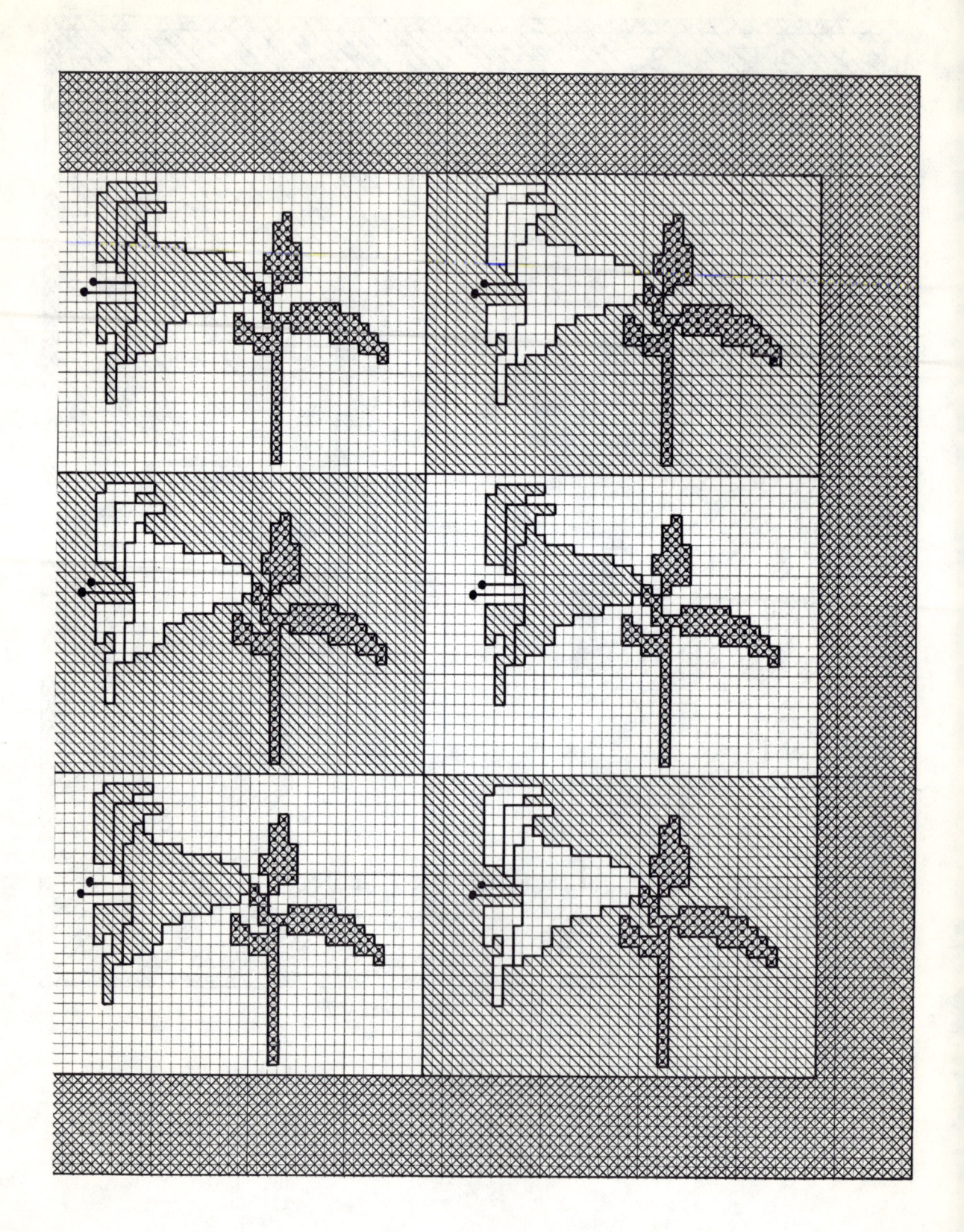

Graph 32

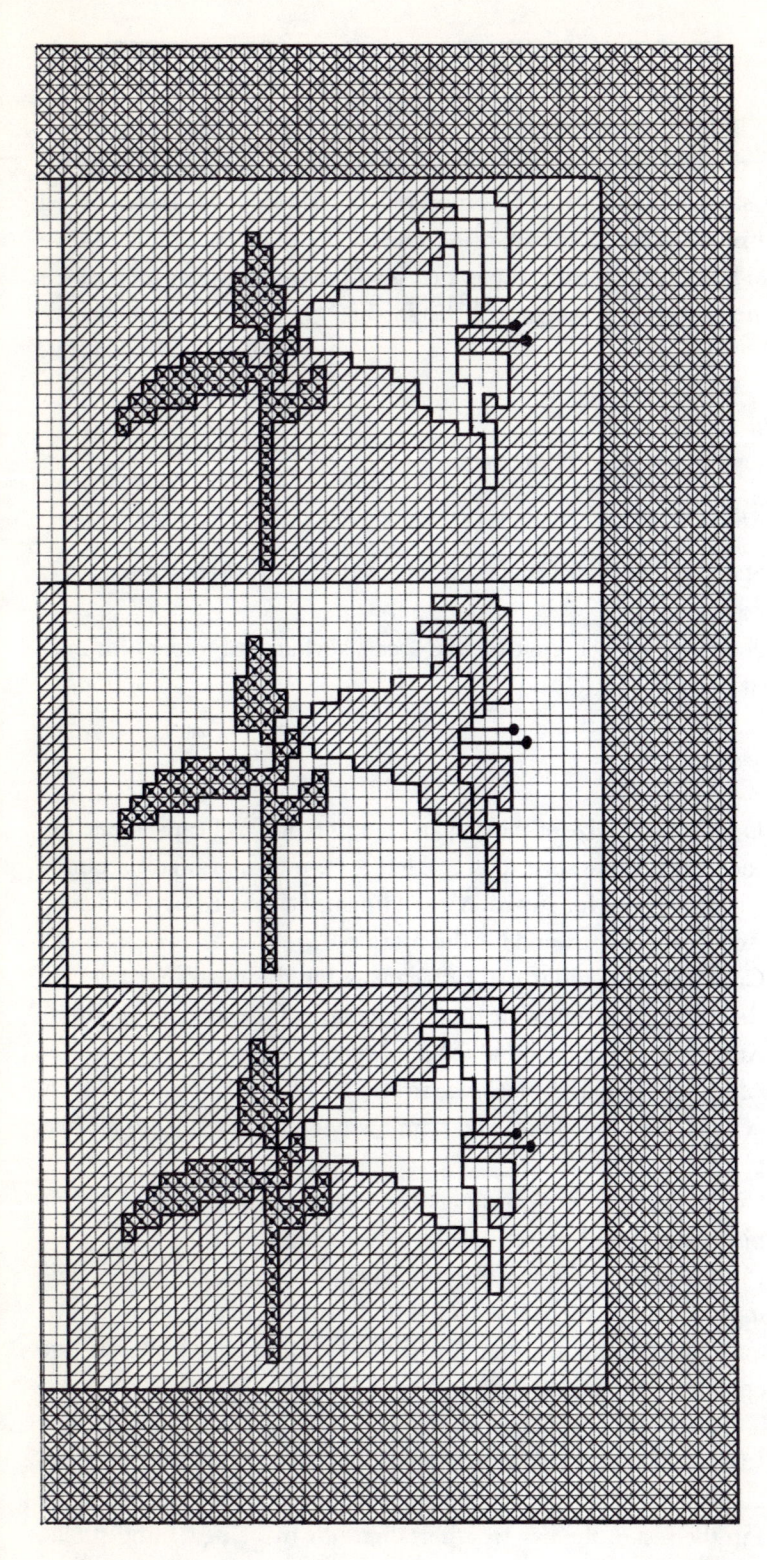

⊠ 7344 medium green

◨ 7318 blue

⊠ 7341 light green

☐ blanc

■ 7433 yellow

See Color Plate.

32

Lilies (Tote Bag)

Consider the lilies how they grow: they toil not, they spin not; and yet I say unto you, that Solomon in all his glory was not arrayed like one of these. If then God so clothe the grass, which is to-day in the field, and to-morrow is cast into the oven; how much more will he clothe you, O ye of little faith?

Luke 12:27–28 KJV.

SUGGESTED PROJECTS — needlepoint tote bag, pillow, rug.

ADDITIONAL SUGGESTIONS — Adapt one of the lilies to a pincushion, bookmark, change purse.

SUGGESTED STITCHES — basket weave, French knot for the seeds; surface embroidery for outlines if desired.

DIRECTIONS FOR CONSTRUCTING A TOTE BAG

1) Decide on the size of the bag and cut two pieces of canvas, one for each side. Make sure you have left a 1½-inch margin all around.
2) Cut two pieces for straps. A good finished size is 18 by 1½ inches. Add 1 inch all around for the margin.
3) Cut one rectangular piece of canvas for the gusset (center). It should be 1½ inches wide times the length of the sides and bottom. Add 1½ inches all around for a margin.
4) After stitching and blocking, machine stitch a few rows ½ inch beyond the needlepoint and trim away excess. Do this to all five pieces.
5) Cut lining material (cotton or silk) to the size of each needlepoint piece, adding ½ inch around for seam allowance.
6) Pin lining pieces to matching needlepoint pieces, right sides facing. Machine-stitch close to the outer row of needlepoint. Leave an edge open for turning. On the two side pieces, leave the top open for inserting straps.
7) Turn right sides out. Steam lightly.
8) Insert straps and sew to the top of the sides. Close open sides on all pieces.
9) Pin the rest of the bag together, then sew by using a blind stitch.

33

Jesus Calming the Waters (Wall Plaque)

And, behold, there arose a great tempest in the sea, insomuch that the ship was covered with the waves: but he was asleep. And his disciples came to him, and awoke him, saying, Lord, save us: we perish. And he saith unto them, Why are ye fearful, O ye of little faith? Then he arose, and rebuked the winds and the sea; and there was a great calm. But the men marvelled, saying, What manner of man is this, that even the winds and the sea obey him!

Matthew 8:24–27 KJV.

SUGGESTED PROJECTS   needlepoint wall plaque.

SUGGESTED STITCHES   continental; French knot for eyes.

Graph 33

- ◨ 7307 navy blue
- ⊓ 7469 dark brown
- ■ 7702 sea-foam green
- ⊡ 7400 pale green
- ⊠ 7432 medium brown
- ◩ ecru
- ⊘ blanc
- ⦁ 7170 flesh
- ☐ 7313 sky blue
- ⊡ 7301 pale blue
- ⊠ 7800 icy blue

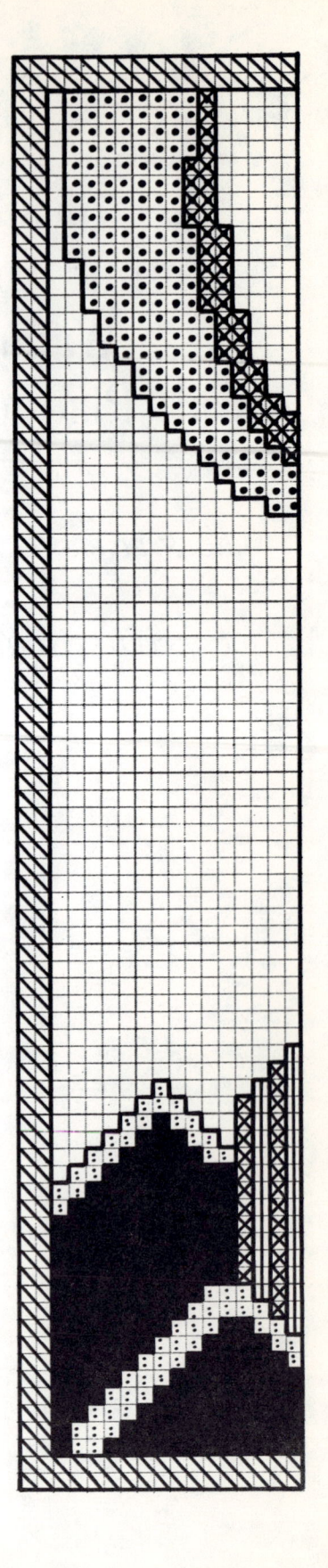

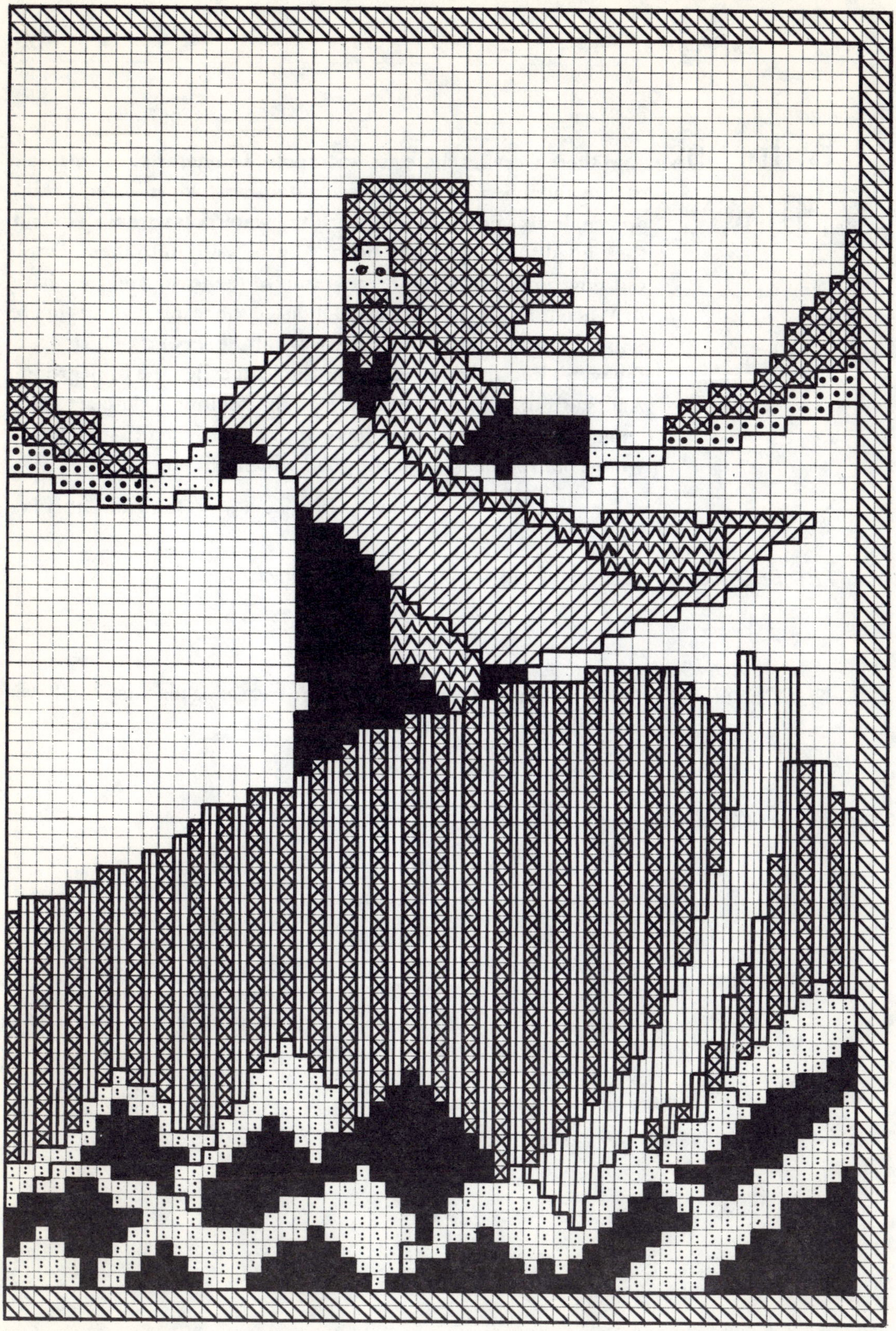

34

Waterpot (Pillow)

And there were set there six waterpots of stone, after the manner of the purifying of the Jews, containing two or three firkins apiece. Jesus saith unto them, Fill the waterpots with water. And they filled them up to the brim. And he saith unto them, Draw out now, and bear unto the governor of the feast. And they bare it. When the ruler of the feast had tasted the water that was made wine, and knew not whence it was: (but the servants which drew the water knew;) the governor of the feast called the bridegroom. And saith unto him, Every man at the beginning doth set forth good wine; and when men have well drunk, then that which is worse: but thou hast kept the good wine until now.

John 2:6–10 KJV.

SUGGESTED PROJECTS needlepoint pillow, tote bag, chair-cushion cover.

ADDITIONAL SUGGESTIONS Adapt a group of these to a rug design, repeating the same motif over and over.

SUGGESTED STITCHES basket weave or upright cross-stitch.

Graph 34

- ⊡ 7538 dark brown
- ◨ 7208 dark red
- ■ 7521 sandy beige
- ☐ 7167 light brown/red
- ◪ 7491 light beige

35

Fish (Tote)

But they answered, "All we have with us is five loaves and two fish." "Bring them here to me," he said. He gave orders that the people were to sit down on the grass; then he took the five loaves and the two fish, raised his eyes to heaven and said the blessing. And breaking the loaves he handed them to his disciples who gave them to the crowds. They all ate as much as they wanted, and they collected the scraps remaining, twelve baskets full. Those who ate numbered about five thousand men, to say nothing of women and children.

Matthew 14:17–21.

SUGGESTED PROJECTS   needlepoint tote, pillow, rug, chair cushion.

ADDITIONAL SUGGESTIONS   The design is twelve boxes to one unit. Consider it as a module. It can be repeated vertically or horizontally.

SUGGESTED STITCHES   continental, mosaic.

For directions to make a tote bag, See LILIES TOTE, Graph #32.

Graph 35

- ☐ 7255 light burgundy
- ⌧ 7341 bright green
- ⊟ 7345 dark green
- ⧄ 7369 light sea-foam green
- ■ 7386 medium sea-foam green
- ⊠ 7340 light bright green

36

Jesus and the Children (Wall Plaque)

People even brought little children to him, for him to touch them; but when the disciples saw this they turned them away. But Jesus called the children to him and said, "Let the little children come to me, and do not stop them; for it is to such as these that the kingdom of God belongs. I tell you solemnly, anyone who does not welcome the kingdom of God like a little child will never enter it."

Luke 18:15–17.

SUGGESTED PROJECTS   needlepoint wall plaque, pillow; can be adapted to a cross-stitch plaque.

SUGGESTED STITCHES   continental or basket weave; surface embroidery for features and outlines.

Graph 36

Symbol	Code	Color	Symbol	Code	Color
⊡	7170	flesh	⊙	7535	dark brown
□	7313	sky blue	◎	7342	green
◺	7727	pale yellow	⊠	7257	mauve
◹	7445	red	■	7317	blue
⊠	7489	brown	◩	7253	light burgundy

89

37

Prodigal Son (Banner)

So he left the place and went back to his father.

While he was still a long way off, his father saw him and was moved with pity. He ran to the boy, clasped him in his arms and kissed him tenderly. Then his son said, "Father, I have sinned against heaven and against you. I no longer deserve to be called your son." But the father said to his servants, "Quick! Bring out the best robe and put it on him; put a ring on his finger and sandals on his feet. Bring the calf we have been fattening, and kill it; we are going to have a feast, a celebration, because this son of mine was dead and has come back to life; he was lost and is found." And they began to celebrate.

Luke:20–24.

SUGGESTED PROJECTS   needlepoint banner.

SUGGESTED STITCHES   continental or basket weave; surface embroidery for features and outlines.

Graph 37

Symbol	Code	Color
⊡	7472	yellow/gold
⊠	7501	wheat
⊠	7490	brown
⊡	7170	flesh
⊙	7715	light gray
■	7419	dark brown
⏐	7115	dark red
□	7799	blue

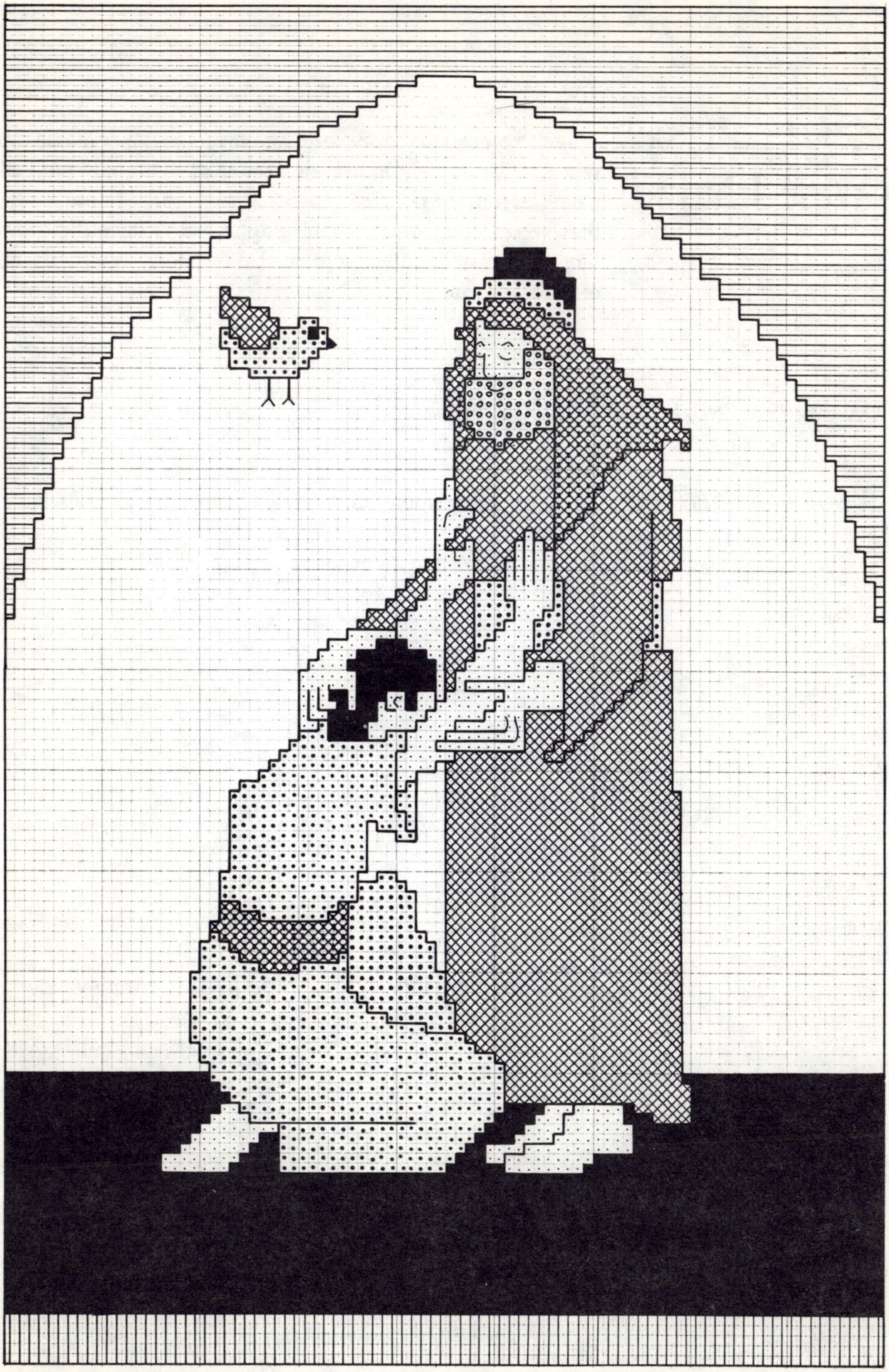

38

Pentecost (Wall Plaque)

When Pentecost day came around, they had all met in one room, when suddenly they heard what sounded like a powerful wind from heaven, the noise of which filled the entire house in which they were sitting, and something appeared to them that seemed like tongues of fire; these separated and came to rest on the head of each of them.

Acts 2:1–3.

SUGGESTED PROJECTS needlepoint plaque.

SUGGESTED STITCHES basket weave or continental, mosaic for border; surface embroidery for outlines.

Graph 38

Symbol	Code	Color	Symbol	Code	Color
⊠	7799	light blue	⊡	7973	bright yellow
⊠	7797	bright blue	⊠	7401	nutmeg brown
⊡	7820	dark bright blue	⊠	7538	brown
⊠	7137	red	⊟	7303	dark red/brown
☐	7170	flesh	⊠	7078	pale yellow
■	7947	orange	⊠	7360	medium brick red

See Color Plate.

39

Heaven's Gates (Plaque)

And I saw a new heaven and a new earth: for the first heaven and the first earth were passed away; and there was no more sea. And I John saw the holy city, new Jerusalem, coming down from God out of heaven, prepared as a bride adorned for her husband. And I heard a great voice out of heaven saying, Behold, the tabernacle of God is with men, and he will dwell with them, and they shall be his people, and God himself shall be with them, and be their God. And God shall wipe away all tears from their eyes; and there shall be no more death, neither sorrow, nor crying, neither shall there be any more pain: for the former things are passed away. And he that sat upon the throne said, Behold, I make all things new. And he said unto me, Write: for these words are true and faithful.

Revelation 21:1–5 KJV.

SUGGESTED PROJECTS　　needlepoint wall plaque, rug.

SUGGESTED STITCHES　　basket weave or continental; latch hook for rug.

Graph 39

■	7823	dark blue	⊡	7503	golden beige
⊠	7591	dark gray/blue	⊟	7411	beige
⊡	7715	light gray	◩	7726	light yellow
◨	7594	medium gray	⊙	7786	medium yellow
☐		silver lame	⊠	7255	pale burgundy

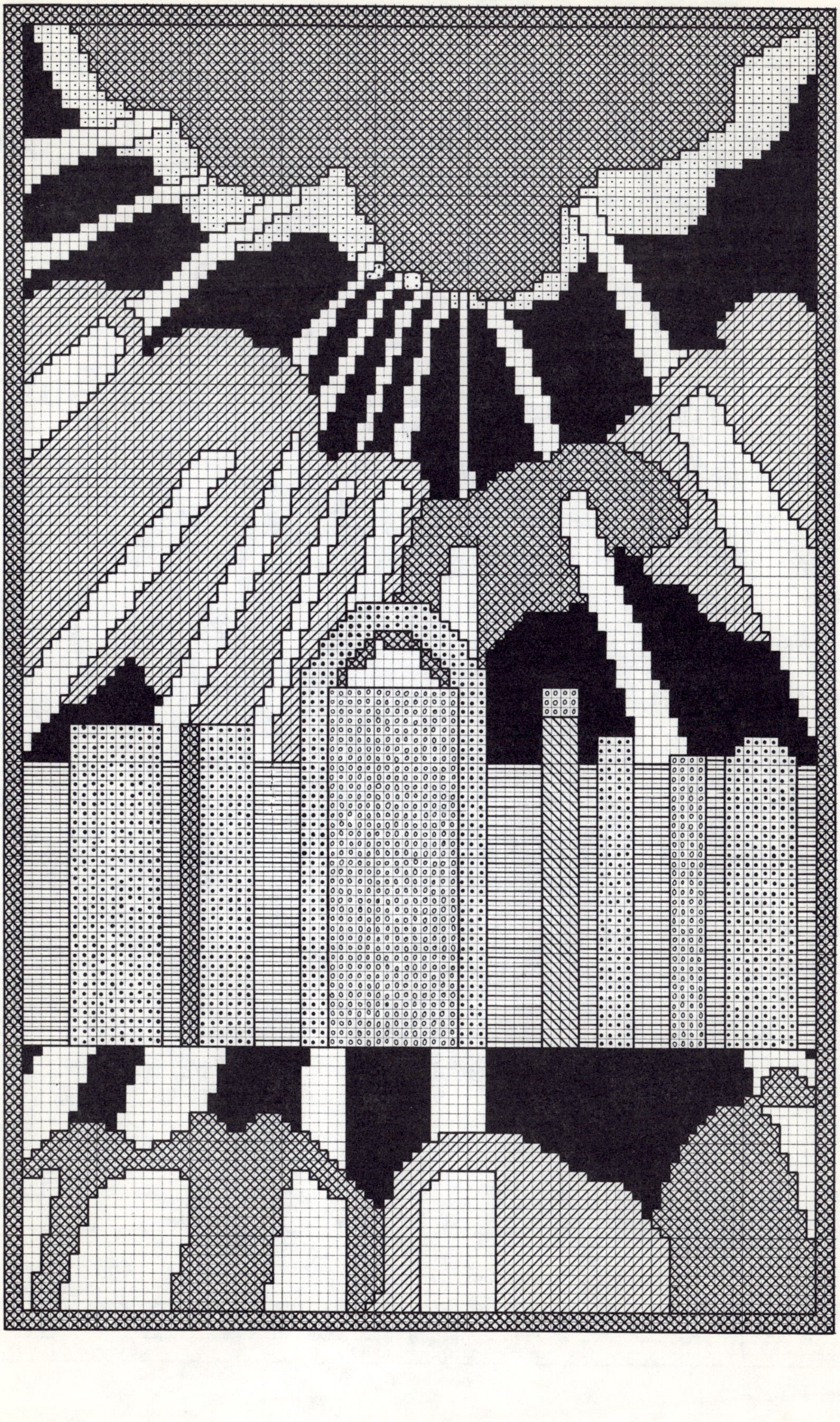

See Color Plate.

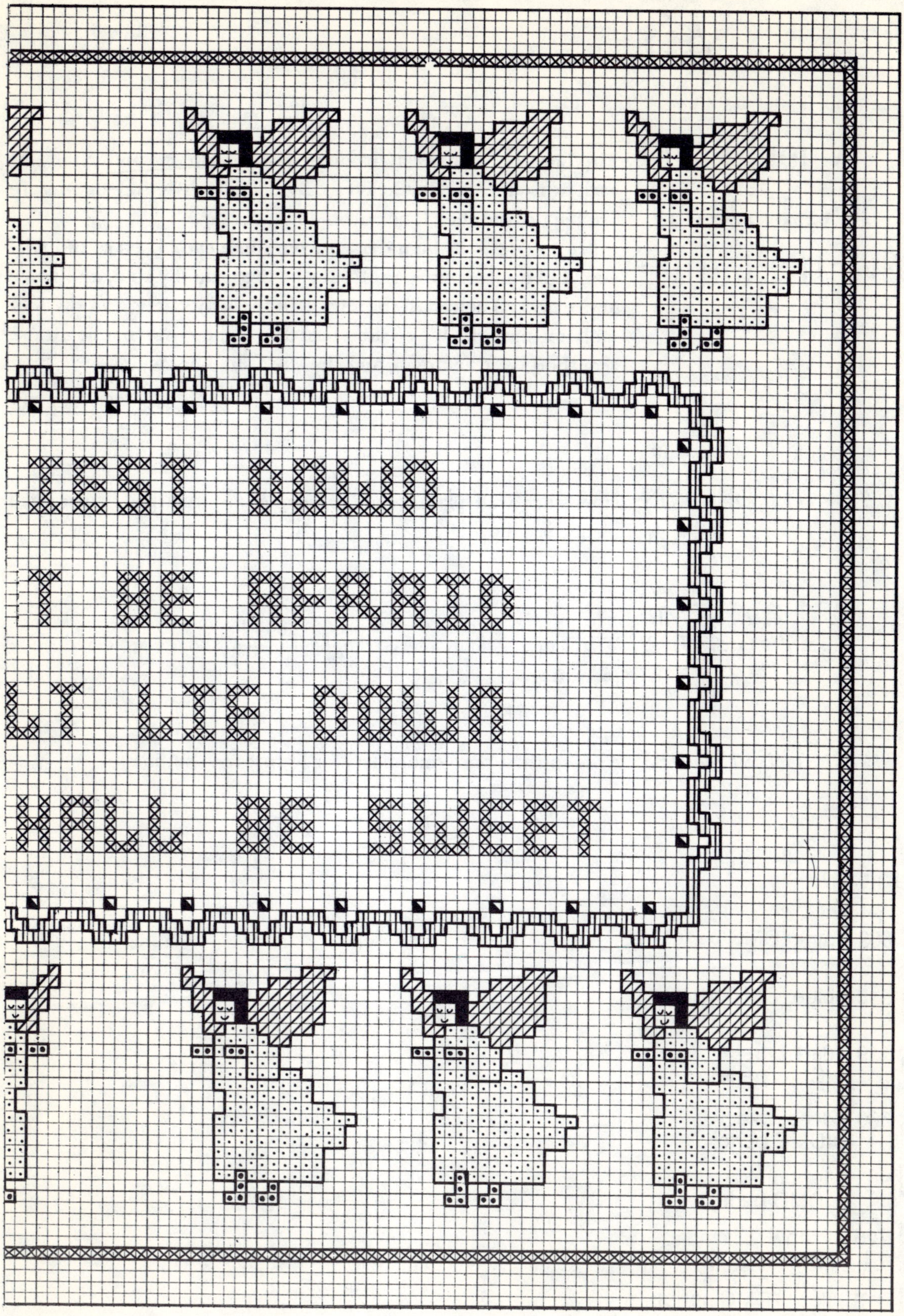
IEST DOWN
T BE AFRAID
LT LIE DOWN
HALL BE SWEET

40

"When Thou Liest Down" (Wall Plaque)

The Lord by wisdom hath founded the earth; by understanding hath he established the heavens. By his knowledge the depths are broken up and the clouds drop down the dew.

My son, let not them depart from thine eyes; keep sound wisdom and discretion: So shall they be life unto thy soul, and grace to thy neck. Then shalt thou walk in thy way safely, and thy foot shall not stumble. When thou liest down, thou shalt not be afraid; yea, thou shalt lie down, and thy sleep shall be sweet.

Proverbs 3:19–24 KJV.

SUGGESTED PROJECTS — cross-stitch wall plaque; can be adapted to needlepoint for a wall plaque or pillow.

ADDITIONAL SUGGESTIONS — The lettering and angels can be isolated and embroidered on a pillowcase.

SUGGESTED STITCHES — cross-stitch; surface embroidery for features and outlines.

Graph 40

- ⊠ 602 pink (DMC perle)
- ⊡ 518 blue (DMC perle)
- ◨ 519 dark blue (DMC perle)
- ⊟ 600 deep rose (DMC perle)
- ◣ 963 light pink (DMC perle)
- ■ 725 yellow (DMC perle)
- ⊙ 819 flesh (DMC perle)

Bibliography

Ambuter, Caroline, *Caroline Ambuter's Needlepoint Celebrations.* New York: Workman Publishing Co., Quadrangle/New York Times, 1976

Archer, K., and Feeley, P., *Perfect Needlepoint Projects from Start to Finish.* New York: St. Martin's Press, 1977

Burchette, Dorothy, *Needlework: Blocking and Finishing.* New York: Charles Scribner's Sons, 1974

Christiansen, Jo Ippolito, *The Needlepoint Book.* Englewood Cliffs, N.J.: Prentice-Hall, 1976.

Lightbody, Donna, *Introducing Needlepoint.* New York: Lothrop, Lee & Shepard, 1973

Miller, Irene, and Lubell, Winifred, *The Stitchery Book.* Garden City, N.Y.: Doubleday, 1975

Wilson, Erica, *Erica Wilson's Embroidery Book.* New York: Charles Scribner's Sons, 1973

JUDITH KALINA is the owner and operator of Fable Soft Sculpture, Inc., in Shenorock. Her fabric art is internationally known, being shown and sold in such gift shops as those in the Louvre and the Brooklyn Museum; and her work has appeared in major women's magazines. Mrs. Kalina has an MFA from Brooklyn College and is the author of *Creating in Cloth*.